Level 4

Building
VOCABULARY
from Word Roots

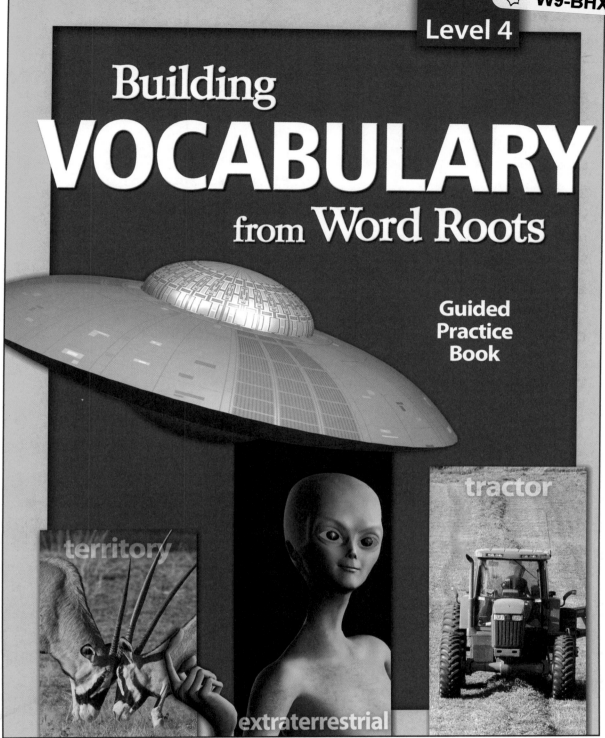

Guided Practice Book

Authors

Timothy Rasinski, Nancy Padak, Rick M. Newton, and Evangeline Newton

Teacher Created Materials

Credits

Editor
Christine Dugan, M.A. Ed.

Assistant Editor
Leslie Huber, M.A.

Senior Editor
Lori Kamola, M.S. Ed.

Editor-in-Chief
Sharon Coan, M.S. Ed.

Editorial Manager
Gisela Lee, M.A.

Creative Director
Lee Aucoin

Designer
Deb Brown

Imaging
Robin Erickson
Phil Garcia
Don Tran

ELL Consultants
Carmen Zuñiga Dunlap, Ph.D.
Associate Dean, College of Education
California State University, Fullerton

Karie A. Feldner, M.S. Ed.

Maria Elvira Gallardo, M.A.

Publisher
Rachelle Cracchiolo M.S. Ed.

To order additional copies of this book or any other Teacher Created Materials products, go to www.tcmpub.com or call 1-800-858-7339.

Teacher Created Materials
5301 Oceanus Drive
Huntington Beach, CA 92649-1030
http://www.tcmpub.com
ISBN 978-1-4938-0648-5
© 2014 Teacher Created Materials, Inc.

Table of Contents

Part A:
Meet the Root

Divide and Conquer

Directions: "Divide" words and then "conquer" them by writing the meaning of the prefix, base, and/or suffix in the blanks. Then select the best definition. The Root Bank lists the meanings of prefixes, bases, and suffixes.

		prefix	base word	definition
1.	export	ex~	Port	G
2.	biweekly	bi~	weely	D
3.	infinite	in~	finite	C
4.	preview	pr	eview	I
5.	rewrite	re	write	B
6.	tricycle	tri	icycle	E

		base	suffix	definition
7.	tasteless	taste	less~	H
8.	beautiful	beauti	autaful	A
9.	quicker	quick	icker	J
10.	kindest	Kind	niest~	F

Definitions

A. lovely; pretty; delighting the eye or senses
B. to write again; to change or revise a text
C. endless
D. occurring two times a week; or, occurring every two weeks
E. a three-wheeled vehicle
F. most gentle and nice
G. to carry or convey goods out of an area
H. lacking taste or flavor
I. to see beforehand
J. more rapid; faster

Part B:
Combine and Create

Three-Syllable Compound Words

Directions: Here are some compound words with three syllables. Circle the first word in the compound word. Then write the compound word on the chart.

fingernail	firefighter	honeybee	lawnmower
trailblazer	watercolor	uppercase	lowercase

First word has one syllable	First word has two syllables
Trail blazer	hony bee
Second word has long vowel sound	**Second word has short vowel sound**
lawn mower	water coler

Part C:
Read and Reason

What's the Difference?

Directions: Work with a partner. Write about the differences between these pairs of words.

Word Pair	Differences
pretest retest	A pretest is a test you take before you lern somthing. A retest is a test you take agin.
preview review	Preview means to look before and Review menes to look agin.
refold unfold	Unfold means to take somthing apart and refold Means to fold something agin.
precook recook	Precook means to cook before and recook Means to cook agin.

Part D:
Extend and Explore

Making and Writing Words

Directions: Use the vowels and consonants to make words that fit the clues. The secret word at the end uses all the letters.

> Consonants: l, s, s, s, t, t   Vowels: a, e, e

1. Past tense of sit _s a t_

2. Another word for exam _t e s t_

3. Opposite of lad _l a s s_

4. To notice the flavor of something; a sense _t e s t e_

5. To decide; to calm or quiet _s e t t l e_

Secret Word: having no #4

_I a s t l e s s_

Part E:
Go for the Gold!

Sixteen Square Wordo

Directions: This game is like Bingo. First, choose a free box and mark it with an X. Then choose words from the word list provided by your teacher and write one word in each box. You can choose the box for each word. Then, your teacher will give a clue for each word. Make an X in the box for each word you match to the clue. If you get four words in a row, column, diagonal, or four corners, call out, "Wordo!"

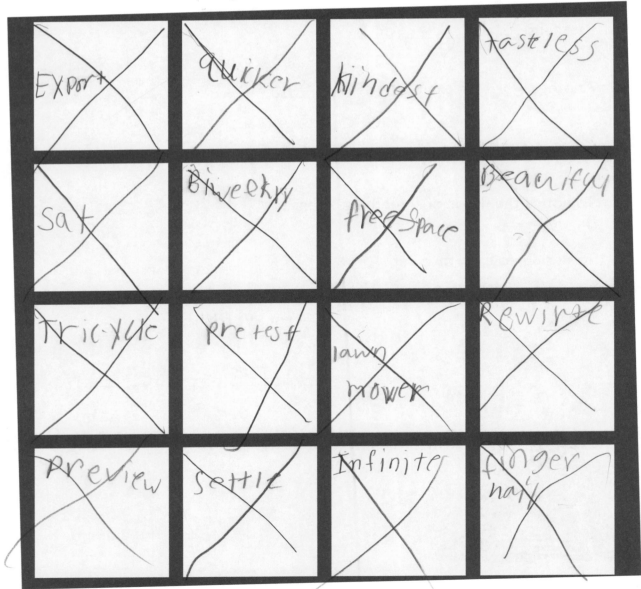

Part A:
Meet the Root

Divide and Conquer

Directions: "Divide" words and then "conquer" them by writing the meaning of the prefix in the blanks. Then select the best definition. Base meanings are provided. Every word in this list begins with the directional prefixes *in-, im-*, meaning "in, on, into."

		prefix	base word	definition
1.	inspect	In	*spect* = look, watch	A
2.	inhale	In	*hale* = breathe	F
3.	induct	In	*duct* = lead	h
4.	inhabit	In	*habit* = dwell, live	E
5.	import	Im	*port* = carry	I
6.	ingest	In	*gest* = carry	J
7.	imprison	Im	prison, jail	C
8.	impulse	Im	*pulse* = push, drive	g
9.	input	In	put	D
10.	invoke	In	*voke* = voice, call	B

Definitions

A. to look into and examine
B. to call on (a deity, a higher power)
C. to place in jail
D. something that is put in; information put in a computer
E. to occupy; to live in
F. to take a breath; to breathe in
G. an urge that drives a person on to act without thinking
H. to lead into the army, a hall of fame, or a club
I. to carry or convey goods into an area
J. to swallow or absorb; to take into one's body

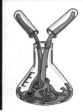

Part B:
Combine and Create

Chart the Words

Directions: Which bases make real words when joined with *in-* and *im-*?
Put these parts together and place them on the chart.

clude	merse	vent	press	side
spect	habit	plode	port	

in-	im-

Work with a partner. Look at the words listed in the two columns of the chart.
Create a rule that will help you know whether you should add *in-* or *im-*.

_____

_____

_____

_____

Part C:
Read and Reason

Word Knowledge

Directions: Read the following story and answer the questions.

In the United States, a new president is inaugurated every four years. It is this person's job to include all people in making decisions about what is best for the country. This person gives speeches and should include immigrants in the ideas that are discussed. Imports should be talked about, too. Overall, the speech is impressive.

1. From the story, what do you think *in-* means? How do you know?

   _____

   _____

2. Use your definition of *in-* to explain what it means to *inaugurate* a president.

   _____

   _____

3. Also from the story, what do you think *im-* means? How do you know?

   _____

   _____

4. Use your definition of *im-* to explain what the word *immigrants* means.

   _____

   _____

5. Can you think of other words that start with *in-* or *im-* ? What are they?

   _____

   _____

6. Can you use one of those words in a sentence? _____

   _____

Part D:
Extend and Explore

Crossword Puzzle

Directions: Read the clues below. Solve the puzzle.

Across
1. official examination or review
2. one who brings things in from another country
3. to look at closely
4. the opposite of leaving out
6. a person who comes up with new ideas
7. to breath in
8. the act of inhaling

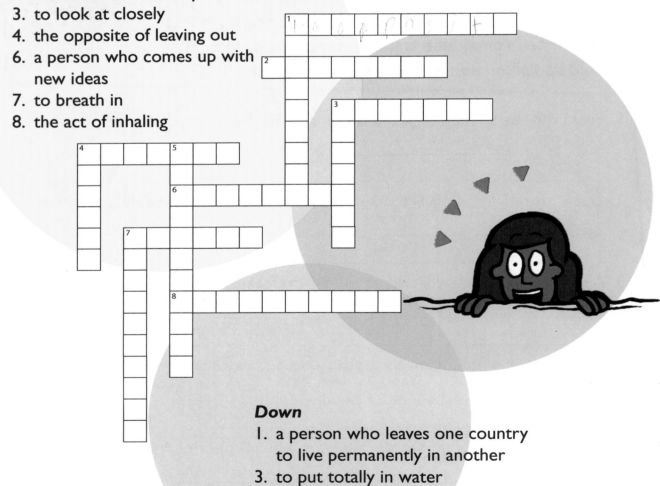

Down
1. a person who leaves one country to live permanently in another
3. to put totally in water
4. the opposite of outside
5. a vacant home or place of residence
7. another word for something that is amazing

Part E:
Go for the Gold!

Word Search

Directions: Find and circle the words in the puzzle. Answers can be across, down, diagonal, or backwards.

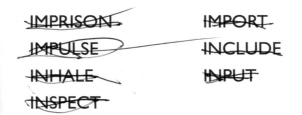

IMPRISON   IMPORT
IMPULSE   INCLUDE
INHALE   INPUT
INSPECT

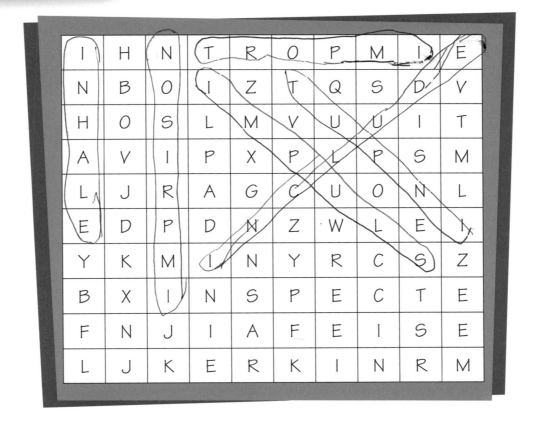

I	H	N	T	R	O	P	M	I	E
N	B	O	I	Z	T	Q	S	D	V
H	O	S	L	M	V	U	U	I	T
A	V	I	P	X	P	L	P	S	M
L	J	R	A	G	C	U	O	N	L
E	D	P	D	N	Z	W	L	E	I
Y	K	M	I	N	Y	R	C	S	Z
B	X	I	N	S	P	E	C	T	E
F	N	J	I	A	F	E	I	S	E
L	J	K	E	R	K	I	N	R	M

Part A:
Meet the Root

Divide and Conquer

Directions: "Divide" words and then "conquer" them by writing the meaning of the prefix in the blanks. Then select the best definition. Base meanings are provided. Every word in this list begins with the directional prefixes *com-, col-*, meaning "with, together."

		prefix	base word	definition
1.	college	col	*leg* = read	D
2.	collide	col	*lid* = slide	H
3.	collect	col	*lect* = gather	E
4.	compact	com	*pact* = congeal, fasten	A
5.	compress	com	*press* = press	J
6.	composition	com	*posit* = put	I
7.	combine	com	*bin* = pair	C
8.	compete	com	*pet* = seek	F
9.	complete	com	*plet* = fill	B
10.	collateral	co	*later* = side	g

Definitions

A. small; tightly packed together
B. to fulfill; to finish
C. to pair together
D. an institution of higher learning in which students read together
E. to gather together and assemble
F. to vie with another for a prize; to engage in a contest
G. occurring along the side; not central
H. to crash or clash
I. arrangement; essay; a musical creation
J. to press or squeeze together

Part B:
Combine and Create

Making Words

Directions: Make words with these word parts. Some boxes may have more than one word. Others may be empty.

	cen	fer	pos	pa
con-				
com-				

DID YOU KNOW?

When ancient Romans borrowed money, they would bring something called *collateral*. If the borrower did not pay back the full amount, the lender got to keep the collateral. Thanks to the Romans, we have the same practice today.

Part C:
Read and Reason

Words in a Poem

Directions: Circle each word with the prefix *com-* or *col-*.

Crazy Construction of a Vocabulary Poem

Connie the cow and Comet the cat
constructed a house just like that.
They conferred and concocted a plan with a chat
and combined their ideas for a four-room flat.
One room for conferences,
another for a study,
Rooms three and four for these two
good buddies.
Connie the cow and Comet the cat
constructed a house in nothing flat.
It's a little house,
compressed and compact.

Now pick three of the words you circled.
Write those words and tell what they mean.

1. combined - to put together
   compressed - press or squeeze

2. co

3. compact - small tightly packed together

Part D:
Extend and Explore

Word Search

Directions: Find and circle the words in the word search puzzles. Answers can be across, down, diagonal, or backwards.

U	E	R	T	K	E	B	I	R	L	C	C	F	K	E
D	C	C	I	Y	I	M	K	J	O	C	O	C	I	T
V	I	W	N	C	I	R	T	N	E	C	N	O	C	A
C	F	F	X	E	C	M	C	G	R	B	G	N	E	G
E	O	P	Y	O	R	E	Z	O	Q	S	R	D	G	E
K	S	N	N	X	N	E	T	M	F	Z	E	U	G	R
F	D	F	C	T	L	C	F	R	D	C	G	C	E	G
M	E	V	R	O	U	B	R	N	G	C	A	T	R	N
R	W	A	U	D	C	E	O	A	O	I	T	X	Q	O
G	T	D	N	A	X	T	X	G	A	C	I	D	O	C
E	K	O	D	D	Y	N	J	B	M	Y	O	B	F	P
L	C	Q	S	U	B	K	U	M	L	Z	N	C	R	L
M	M	C	R	L	S	M	U	Q	Q	E	N	K	T	Y
H	Z	O	D	A	G	T	W	B	R	E	T	L	P	E
C	O	N	S	T	R	U	C	T	O	L	N	U	D	S

CONCENTRATE

CONCENTRIC

CONCOCT

CONDUCT

CONDUCTOR

CONFER

CONFERENCE

CONGREGATE

CONGREGATION

CONSTRUCT

COLLABORATE

COLLATE

COLLATERAL

COLLEAGUE

COLLECT

COLLEGE

COLLIDE

COLLISION

COLLOQUIAL

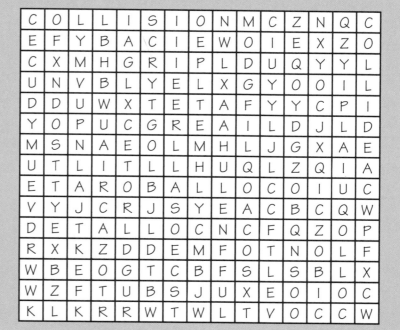

C	O	L	L	I	S	I	O	N	M	C	Z	N	Q	C
E	F	Y	B	A	C	I	E	W	O	I	E	X	Z	O
C	X	M	H	G	R	I	P	L	D	U	Q	Y	Y	L
U	N	V	B	L	Y	E	L	X	G	Y	O	O	I	L
D	D	U	W	X	T	E	T	A	F	Y	Y	C	P	I
Y	O	P	U	C	G	R	E	A	I	L	D	J	L	D
M	S	N	A	E	O	L	M	H	L	J	G	X	A	E
U	T	L	I	T	L	L	H	U	Q	L	Z	Q	I	A
E	T	A	R	O	B	A	L	L	O	C	O	I	U	C
V	Y	J	C	R	J	S	Y	E	A	C	B	C	Q	W
D	E	T	A	L	L	O	C	N	C	F	Q	Z	O	P
R	X	K	Z	D	D	E	M	F	O	T	N	O	L	F
W	B	E	O	G	T	C	B	F	S	L	S	B	L	X
W	Z	F	T	U	B	S	J	U	X	E	O	I	O	C
K	L	K	R	R	W	T	W	L	T	V	O	C	C	W

Part E:
Go for the Gold!

Crossword Puzzle

Directions: Read the clues below. Solve the puzzle.

Across

1. to press together
2. to express oneself in such a way that one is clearly understood
5. a person who is frequently in the company of another
6. to examine to find similarities or differences
7. the combining of distinct parts or elements to form a whole

Down

1. to put together and make as one
3. to create or produce
4. to put together from various sources
5. closely packed together
7. for or by a group rather than individuals

com-
col-

Part A:
Meet the Root

Divide and Conquer

Directions: "Divide" words and then "conquer" them by writing the meaning of the prefix in the blanks. Then select the best definition. Base meanings are provided. Every word in this list begins with the directional prefix *de-*, meaning "down, off of."

	prefix	base word	definition
1. descend	de	*scend* = climb, step	B
2. depress	de	press	E
3. deposit	de	*posit* = put	I
4. deviate	de	*via* = way, road	F
5. deflate	de	*flat* = air, blow	A
6. deformed	de	*form* = form, shape	H
7. degrease	de	grease	D
8. defrost	de	frost	C
9. defogger	de	fog	J
10. declaw	de	claw	G

Definitions

A. to let out air; to flatten
B. to climb down; to take a lower position
C. to remove ice and frost from
D. to remove grease from
E. to press down

F. to swerve or veer from a path or course
G. to remove claws from
H. disfigured or misshapen
I. to put down money in advance payment
J. a device or chemical that clears the air

Part B:
Combine and Create

Word Sort

Directions: The prefix *de-* can mean "down" or "off of." Put these words on the chart where they belong.

decelerate   declaw   deflate   defrost
deice   deplane   depopulate   dethrone

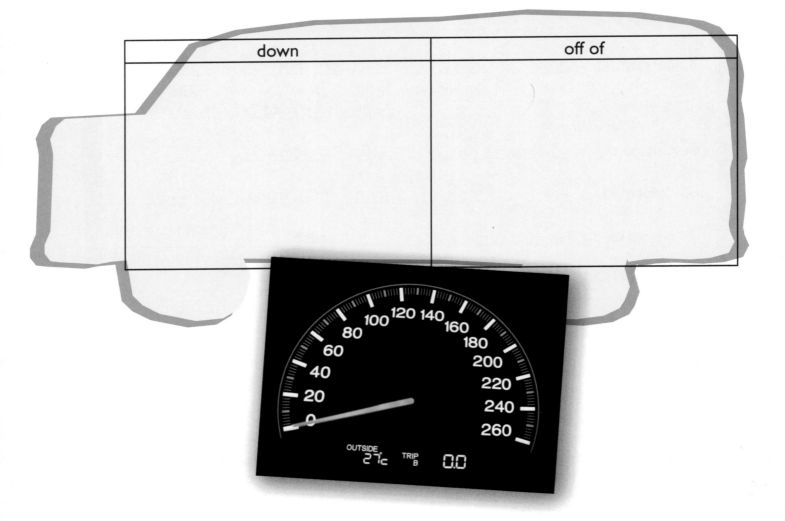

down	off of

Fill in the Blanks

Part C:
Read and Reason

Directions: Fill in the blanks for this story with words that make sense.
Answer the questions when you are finished with the story.

The new bookstore opened at the mall today. It's called
DeBooker's, and it _de bug_ (dethrones, debugs)
the previous store called Bary's and Newman's, which used to rule
the mall as the king of all great bookstores. DeBooker's, however,
is a true ruler because of all of the different kinds of
books it carries.

My mom even drove me over to the mall to check it
out. They have a section on animals that is all about
declawing (defrosting, declawing) any animal
with claws so they can't scratch. One book in the travel section
even tells you how to _deplane_ (deplane, degrease)
from an airplane in case of an emergency.

Another book talks about bike riding, and even gave me some
good information on how to _deflate_ (deflate,
defog) my tires to the proper pressure. My tires are too full of air
and sometimes pop.

Questions:

1. What do you like to read about? _____

   _____

2. Can you recommend a favorite book of yours that DeBooker's should sell?
   Write the title and explain why you think someone might be interested in
   buying it. _____

   _____

Part D:
Extend and Explore

Opposites Attract

Directions: Work with a partner. Write the opposite of these words. Your answers will all begin with *de-*.

Word	Opposite
1. inflate	_____
2. ascend	_____
3. accelerate	_____
4. compose	_____

Now select one of the pairs from above. Figure out a way to show these words in a skit. Use actions in your skit but no words. Perform your skit for another group. See if they can figure out your words.

Part E:
Go for the Gold!

Sixteen Square Wordo

Directions: This game is like Bingo. First, choose a free box and mark it with an X. Then choose words from the word list provided by your teacher and write one word in each box. You can choose the box for each word. Then, your teacher will give a clue for each word. Make an X in the box for each word you match to the clue. If you get four words in a row, column, diagonal, or four corners, call out, "Wordo!"

Part A:
Meet the Root

Divide and Conquer

Directions: "Divide" words and then "conquer" them by writing the meaning of the prefix in the blank. Then select the best definition. Base meanings are provided. Every word in this list begins with the directional prefix *pro-*, meaning "forward, ahead, for, on behalf of."

	prefix	base word	definition
1. promote	pro*mote*	*mot* = move	f
2. progress	pro	*gress* = step	h
3. proceed	pro	*ceed* = go	d
4. propeller	pro	*pel* = push, drive	I
5. proclaim	pro	*claim* = shout	J
6. pronoun	pro	*noun* = name	C
7. pro-war	pro	war	A
8. product	pro	*duct* = lead	b
9. proverb	pro	*verb* = word	E
10. profess	pro	*fess* = speak	g

Definitions
A. in favor of war
B. anything made or produced
C. a word that stands for a noun or a name
D. to go forward; to continue
E. a wise saying; an expression of wisdom in few words
F. to move forward to the next grade or level; to advance
G. to declare and affirm; to claim to be an expert
H. advancement; the act of moving ahead
I. rotating device that drives a vehicle forward
J. to announce publicly; to shout forth

Part B:
Combine and Create

Word Sort

Directions: Sometimes *pro-* means "for" or "in favor of," and sometimes it doesn't. Put these *pro-* words on the chart where they belong.

pro-war   pro-peace   progress   promise   pro-business
promotion   pro-environment   propeller   pronoun   proceed

means "in favor of"	does not mean "in favor of"

DID YOU KNOW?

The most famous *proclamation* in American history is the Emancipation Proclamation. In 1863, President Abraham Lincoln proclaimed that "all slaves in any state shall be forever free." By doing so, the president helped America live up to its promise that all people "are created equal." The Emancipation Proclamation was a great moment in American history. It will always be one of Abraham Lincoln's greatest achievements.

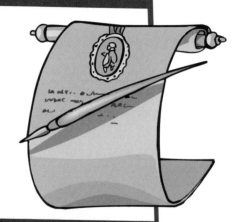

Part C:
Read and Reason

Writing Sentences

Directions: Write sentences that include both of the listed words.

1. propeller/progress _____

   _____

   _____

2. promise/propel _____

   _____

   _____

3. pronoun/produce _____

   _____

   _____

4. proceed/proclaim _____

   _____

   _____

5. pro-war/pro-peace _____

   _____

   _____

Part D:
Extend and Explore

Word Ladder: Propose

Directions:　Climb the word ladder by reading the clues and then writing the correct words.

Propose

1. Remove the *pro-* in *propose* to make a word that describes what models do.　　_____

2. Change one letter to make a long, thick piece of wood.　　_____

3. Change one letter to make the opposite of future.　　_____

4. Change one letter to make a tall pole that holds sails on a boat.　　_____

5. Change one letter to make another word for market or store.　　_____

6. Change one letter to make a girl's name.　　_____

7. Add one letter to tell what happens to people who do #1.　　_____

Part E:
Go for the Gold!

Sixteen Square Wordo

Directions: This game is like Bingo. First, choose a free box and mark it with an X. Then choose words from the word list provided by your teacher and write one word in each box. You can choose the box for each word. Then, your teacher will give a clue for each word. Make an X in the box for each word you match to the clue. If you get four words in a row, column, diagonal, or four corners, call out, "Wordo!"

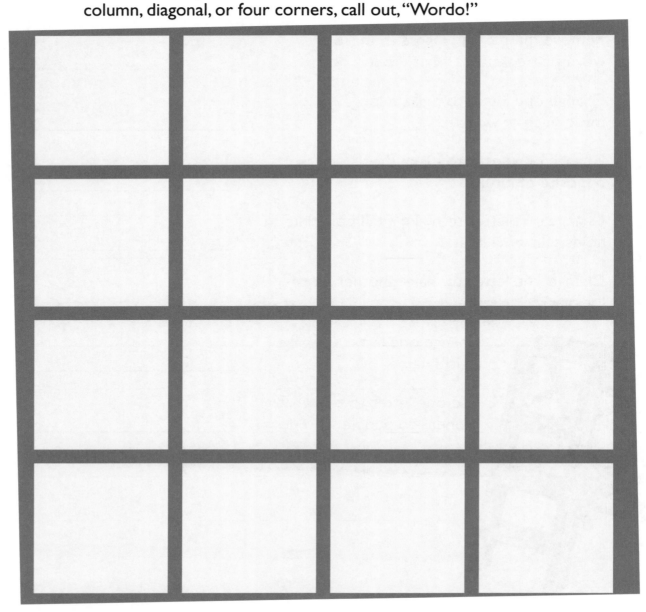

Part A:
Meet the Root

Divide and Conquer

Directions: Your teacher will give you a list of words. "Divide" each word into a prefix and a base. Then "conquer" them by writing the meaning of the words.

	word	prefix means	base means	definition
1.	_____	_____	_____	_____
2.	_____	_____	_____	_____
3.	_____	_____	_____	_____
4.	_____	_____	_____	_____
5.	_____	_____	_____	_____
6.	_____	_____	_____	_____
7.	_____	_____	_____	_____
8.	_____	_____	_____	_____
9.	_____	_____	_____	_____
10.	_____	_____	_____	_____

Part B:
Combine and Create

Word Sort

Directions: First, take the prefix off each word. Then put the rest of the word on the chart where it belongs. Decide if the remaining letters form a word.

inside	inhale	implode	concoct
construct	community	compress	colony
collect	dethrone	detach	deflate

is a word	is not a word

Part C:
Read and Reason

Making New Words

Directions: Add *con-, com-,* or *col-* to these word parts to make new words. Then use each new word in a sentence.

1. *bine:* _____

   Sentence: _____

   _____

2. *coct:* _____

   Sentence: _____

   _____

3. *duct:* _____

   Sentence: _____

   _____

4. *lect:* _____

   Sentence: _____

   _____

5. *lide:* _____

   Sentence: _____

   _____

6. *pose:* _____

   Sentence: _____

   _____

Part D:
Extend and Explore

Word Search

Directions: Find and circle the words in the puzzle. Answers can be across, down, diagonal, or backwards.

COLLABORATE	COLLISION	COLONY
COMBINE	COMMUNE	COMPANION
CONCENTRATE	CONGREGATE	CONSTRUCT
DECLAW	DEICE	DEPRESS
IMPLODE	INAUGURATE	INSPECTOR

A	E	T	D	F	K	D	Z	O	U	C	I	R	D	C
C	S	D	D	V	E	E	N	W	O	O	E	O	E	O
R	O	Y	O	I	E	H	L	L	J	N	N	T	C	M
S	R	L	C	L	R	T	L	Y	L	C	I	C	L	P
K	U	E	O	A	P	A	A	G	F	E	B	E	A	A
C	W	K	V	N	B	M	D	G	K	N	M	P	W	N
G	E	Q	Q	O	Y	V	I	Y	E	T	O	S	C	I
E	T	A	R	U	G	U	A	N	I	R	C	N	G	O
A	H	A	N	R	W	Y	J	Y	B	A	G	I	E	N
L	T	C	O	N	S	T	R	U	C	T	P	N	I	A
E	N	O	I	S	I	L	L	O	C	E	U	P	O	I
D	E	P	R	E	S	S	V	R	I	M	K	E	Z	C
O	L	X	L	S	Z	S	W	Y	M	Y	F	P	D	H
T	U	U	B	L	V	I	N	O	V	K	Q	S	G	L
T	Y	Y	L	Z	Z	Z	C	B	B	C	W	A	T	P

Part E:
Go for the Gold!

Crossword Puzzle

Directions: Read the clues and complete the crossword puzzle.

Across

4. to gather
5. to make something never before created
10. the combining of distinct parts or elements to form a whole
13. to separate or unfasten
14. food made by mixing different ingredients

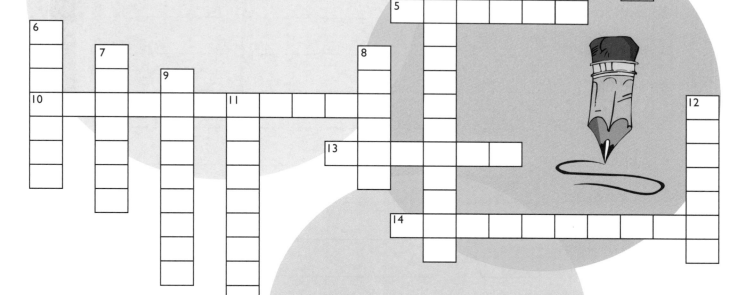

Down

1. words more suitable for speech than writing
2. a group of people living near each other
3. to eat food
4. the act of focusing total attention
6. to go down
7. to press together
8. to discuss
9. one with whom you work
11. permanent residents
12. to leave a plane

Part A:

Meet the Root

Divide and Conquer

Directions: "Divide" words and then "conquer" them by writing the meaning of the base in the blanks. Then select the best definition. Every word in this list is based on the bases *audi-*, *audit-*, meaning "hear, listen." Words #7–10 are compound words with the base *audio-*.

		base means	definition
1.	audit	hear	I
2.	audition	auudition	B
3.	auditorium	aucitorium	F
4.	audible	audible	J
5.	audience	audience	g
6.	auditor	auditor	C
7.	audiovisual	audiovisual	E
8.	audiotape	audiotape	a
9.	audiolingual	audiolingual	D
10.	audiocassette	aulo cassette	h

Definitions

A. tape for recording sound
B. a hearing given to a performer
C. a person authorized to a performer
D. pertaining to the hearing and speaking of language
E. pertaining to hearing and seeing
F. a hall or building for hearing performances and speakers
G. an assembly of hearers or spectators
H. a cassette that plays music or recorded voices
I. to check financial records; to hold a hearing over accounts
J. capable of being heard; sufficiently loud

Part B:
Combine and Create

Word Sort

Directions: Work with a partner. Put these words on the chart under the correct heading. Some words may go in more than one column. Some words may not fit under any heading.

audience	auditorium	audiocassette
audition	inaudible	audiotape
auditory	audible	audiotaped

person	place	thing

Part C:
Read and Reason

Sound Check: A Dialogue

Directions: Circle the *audi* vocabulary words in the following conversation. Imagine that the conversation takes place inside a new auditorium.

Hey, guys. I'm going to test the speakers. Ok?

Yeah.

Can you hear it? Is it audible?

What?

Can you hear the speakers out in the audience?

Yeah. I can hear you.

If you can hear me, wave your hands. I'm in the auditorium . . . .

Questions:

1. From the conversation above, what do you think *audi* means? How do you know? _____

    _____

2. Use your definition of *audi* to explain what *audible* means. _____

    _____

3. Use your definition of *audi* to explain what *audience* means. _____

    _____

4. Now write a sentence that has both *audible* and *auditorium* in it. Share your sentence with a friend. _____

    _____

Part D:
Extend and Explore

Talk It Out

Directions: Work with a partner. Talk about how the meaning of these words has something to do with hearing or listening. Record your ideas below.

audible: Something you can hear or lisen to.

audience: A assembly of hearers.

auditorium: A building fill with loads of pepole.

inaudible: To not hear loadly.

Part E:
Go for the Gold!

Crossword Puzzle

Directions: Read the clues and complete the crossword puzzle.

Across

2. an examined and verified account
4. that is heard or that can be heard
5. a tryout
6. the sense of hearing
7. a large building for public meetings or performances
8. a tape recording of sound
9. both audible and visual

Down

1. the act of hearing or attending
3. impossible to hear
4. able to be heard
5. a way of learning language by listening and speaking

Part A:
Meet the Root

Divide and Conquer

Directions: "Divide" words and then "conquer" them by writing the meaning of the prefix and base in the blanks. Then select the best definition. Words marked with an X have no prefix. Every word in this list is based on the bases *voc, vok, voice*, meaning "voice, call."

	prefix	base word	definition
1. vocal	X	voc	I
2. convoke	con- = with	voke	C
3. revoke	re- = back, against	voke	A
4. invoke	in- = in, on, into	voke	j
5. vocabulary	X	voc	G
6. vocalize	X		e
7. convocation			H
8. vocation	X		F
9. avocation	a- = away, from		B
10. multivocal			D

Definitions

A. to cancel; to annul by recalling
B. a hobby (performed while away from one's calling)
C. a meeting or ceremony that calls people together
D. consisting of many voices; choral

E. to express in voice or in words
F. a profession, job, or calling
G. a list of words
H. to call on (a deity, a higher power)
I. oral; having voice; spoken with the voice
J. to call people together to a meeting

Part B:
Combine and Create

Making Words

Directions: Work with a partner. Select two prefixes from the list below.
Think of as many words as possible that have that prefix and the
base *voc, voke,* or *voice.*

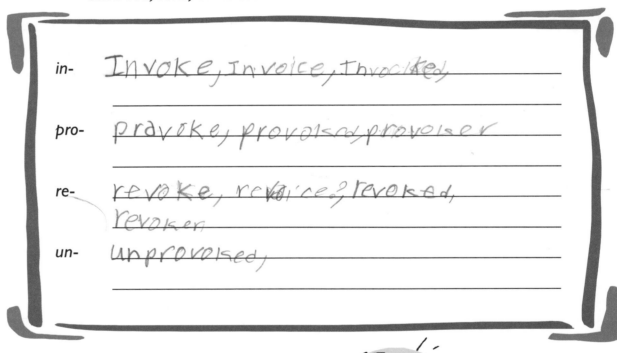

in-   Invoke, Invoice, Invooked,

pro-   Provoke, provoked, provoker

re-   revoke, revoice, revoked, revoker

un-   unprovoked,

DID YOU KNOW?

In Ancient Rome, school children studied out loud in class. As they
learned new words, they would sound them out with their voices.
This is why the English word *vocabulary* (a list of words) is built on
the Latin word for "voice." Students took their vocabulary quizzes by
reciting the words aloud. Even as adults, Romans continued the habit
of reading everything out loud. Roman doctors would often order
sick patients to give up reading for awhile because their reading would
irritate their vocal cords and make a sore throat worse!

Part C:
Read and Reason

Poetry Reading

Directions: Read the poem and answer the questions.

My avocation is collecting
many stamps of all
shapes, sizes, and colors
to show my
friends
the different ideas
in our American history.

Questions:

1. What does *voc* mean in the poem? How do you know? _____

   The word voc meanes to voice
   or call.

2. What is an *avocation*? Do you have an avocation? What is your avocation?

   An avocation is a happay or activity
   you do for fun. My avocaton is to
   play soccer.

   _____

Part D:
Extend and Explore

Word Search

Directions: Find and circle the *voc, voke,* and *voice* words listed below in the word search. Answers can be across, down, diagonal, or backwards.

ADVOCATE   CONVOKE   INVOKED
MULTIVOCAL   PROVOKE   SUBVOCALIZE
VOCABULARY   VOCALS   VOCATION
VOICE

N	V	E	C	V	T	S	C	C	N	Q	V	G	D	B
O	O	F	T	B	Y	U	K	H	O	O	W	E	Q	L
I	C	G	Y	A	O	B	D	U	I	N	K	P	C	I
T	A	A	T	L	C	V	F	C	Y	O	V	R	U	M
A	L	B	E	Y	N	O	E	K	V	U	M	O	U	Z
C	S	C	R	Z	D	C	V	N	Z	Y	M	L	K	U
O	Q	O	L	U	F	A	I	D	I	S	T	Q	A	E
V	C	Y	J	U	I	L	I	P	A	I	L	O	H	V
G	O	Y	C	C	M	I	E	S	V	U	H	L	I	B
K	P	W	C	R	M	Z	F	O	J	Y	O	H	K	I
P	R	O	V	O	K	E	C	H	S	R	K	T	U	I
V	P	A	M	Y	R	A	L	U	B	A	C	O	V	G
V	D	Y	I	G	L	F	D	B	R	H	A	J	E	T
T	W	P	U	E	E	E	Z	V	V	V	K	V	G	E
Q	Q	L	C	M	J	Z	S	J	V	K	C	N	S	W

Part E:
Go for the Gold!

Sixteen Square Wordo

Directions: This game is like Bingo. First, choose a free box and mark it with an X. Then choose words from the word list provided by your teacher and write one word in each box. You can choose the box for each word. Then, your teacher will give a clue for each word. Make an X in the box for each word you match to the clue. If you get four words in a row, column, diagonal, or four corners, call out, "Wordo!"

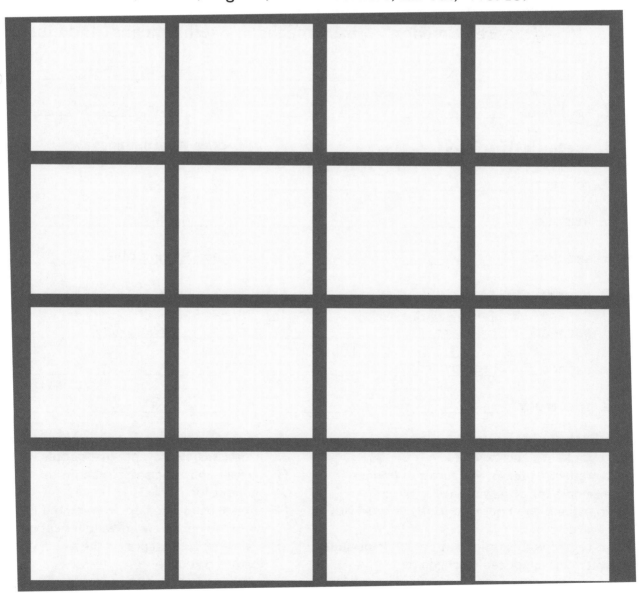

Part A:
Meet the Root

Divide and Conquer

Directions: "Divide" words and then "conquer" them by writing the meaning of the prefix and base suffix in the blanks. Then select the best definition. Words marked with an X have no prefix. Every word in this list is based on the bases *spec, spect*, meaning "watch, look at."

		prefix means	base means	suffix means	definition
1.	spectator	X		*-ator* = one who does	
2.	speculate	X		*-ate* = make or do	
3.	spectacles	X		*-acles* = small things	
4.	respect			X	
5.	inspect			X	
6.	specimen	X		*-imen* = thing, object	
7.	expect			X	
8.	suspect	up from under (assimilated *sub-*)		X	
9.	aspect	to, toward		X	
10.	spectrum	X		X	

Definitions

A. to look into and examine
B. to reflect, observe, and guess; to ponder
C. a sample for observation
D. to esteem and honor; to look back on with regard
E. to regard with suspicion; a person kept under watch for supposed wrongdoing

F. eyeglasses; also, events that people look at
G. to wait and anticipate; to be on the lookout for
H. the full band of colors in refracted light
I. an onlooker; one who watches sports
J. a view or appearance to the eye; a visible feature or quality

Part B:
Combine and Create

Making New Words

Directions: Work with a partner to brainstorm *spec, spect* words that contain these word parts.

in- _____

_____

intro- _____

_____

pro- _____

_____

DID YOU KNOW?

You recognize that the word *expect* begins with the prefix ex-, which means "out." If you are *expecting* something in the mail, you will be "looking out" for the mailman. The Latin base of this word is *spect*. Anyone who is *expecting* something is on the "lookout." In the word *expect*, the "s" has dropped out because the prefix ex- contains a built-in "s" sound. It would be a waste of letters to spell this word as "ex-spect." For this reason, we spell it without the "s" and correctly write *expect*.

DID YOU KNOW?

In American history, we learn about people who rushed to California in the 1800s to search for gold. As they traveled west, they "looked ahead," and tried to find gold in the ground and in rivers. They carried pickaxes to *prospect* for gold in rocks and caves, and they carried sifting pans to *prospect* for gold in the sand beds of rivers and streams. Wherever these people went, they kept their eyes fixed ahead in hopes of being the first to strike a bonanza! They were America's first *prospectors*.

Part C:
Read and Reason

Fill in the Blanks

Directions: Choose words from the Word Bank to fill in the blanks for
the following story.   (Hint: You will use all the words.)

1. After the touchdown, the _Spectator_ cheered and stood up, rallying their team for a comeback victory.

2. The fireworks were _____ displayed in the night sky.

3. The _Spectacles_ she wore made her look smart as well as attractive.

4. She was very _____ when talking with others in class.

5. The policeman informed the man that he should be more _____ about the consequences of his actions.

6. Jenny made a _____ of herself when she tripped down the stairs.

7. His mother _Inspecten_ his homework every night.

8. After being called into the principal's office, her attitude became more _respectful_ toward her teacher.

Word Bank

spectators
spectacularly
introspective
respectful
spectacle
circumspect
spectacles
inspected

Part D:
Extend and Explore

Magic Square

Directions: Match the words and definitions. Put the number of the definition in the correct box. If your answers are correct, each row and column will add up to the same number.

TERMS	DEFINITIONS
A. spectacles	2 someone who watches a sporting event
B. inspect	5 cannot be heard
C. respectful	6 behave with respect
D. spectator	7 list of words
E. prospector	8 look closely
F. bespectacled	9 someone looking for gold
G. spectacular	10 glasses
H. vocabulary	12 eye-catching display
I. inaudible	13 wearing spectacles

A 10	B 8	C 6
D 2	E 9	F 13
G 12	H 7	I 5

Magic Number: 24

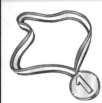

Part E:
Go for the Gold!

Sixteen Square Wordo

Directions: This game is like Bingo. First, choose a free box and mark it with an X. Then choose words from the word list provided by your teacher and write one word in each box. You can choose the box for each word. Then, your teacher will give a clue for each word. Make an X in the box for each word you match to the clue. If you get four words in a row, column, diagonal, or four corners, call out, "Wordo!"

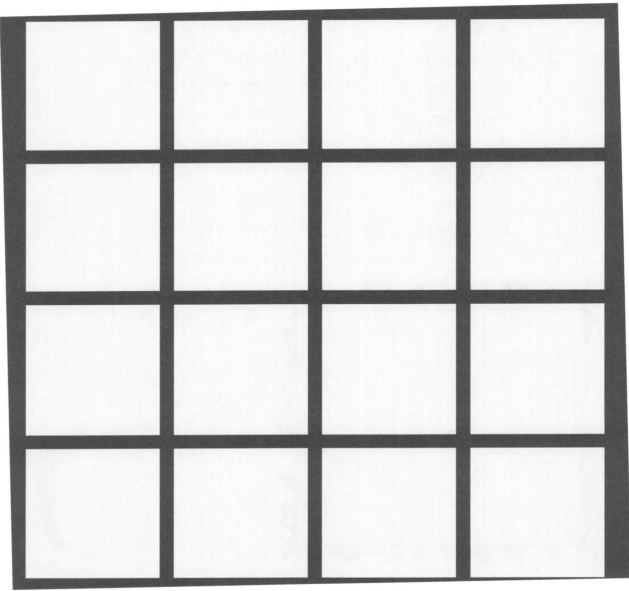

Part A:
Meet the Root

Divide and Conquer

Directions: "Divide" words and then "conquer" them by writing the meaning of the prefix and base in the blanks. Then select the best definition. Words marked with an X have no prefix. Every word in this list is based on the base *terr*, meaning "land, ground, earth." **Hint:** In words #9 and #10, write the meaning of the first base in the prefix blank.

		prefix	base word	definition
1.	terrain	X		
2.	Mediterranean	*medi-* = middle		
3.	terrace	X		
4.	terrarium	X		
5.	subterranean			
6.	extraterrestrial	*extra-* = outside		
7.	territory	X		
8.	terrier	X		
9.	Terre Haute		*haute* = high	
10.	terra-cotta		*cotta* = cooked	

Definitions
A. a region of land belonging to a country
B. the sea in the middle of the Greco-Roman world
C. underground
D. a container for displaying small land animals and plants
E. a species of dog bred for burrowing into the earth
F. fired clay; a type of earthenware
G. a level piece of paved ground; a patio or balcony
H. a tract of land with distinct physical features; topography
I. a city in Indiana named for its high ground
J. occurring in outer space

Part B:
Combine and Create

Word Sort

Directions: Here are words that contain the letters *terr*.
Work with a partner to put them on the chart.

terrible   terror   terrier   terrace   terrain
territory   terrific   terrorist   terrify   terrarium

has to do with "earth"	does not have to do with "earth"

DID YOU KNOW?

Long ago, outdoorsmen bred a special kind of dog to help hunters catch small animals that burrowed underground. This new breed was called a *terrier*. With their square-cut snout, these dogs can chew into a hole in the ground that has been dug by a weasel or small fox. These same dogs also have very strong tails that enable the hunters to pull them out of the holes into which they have burrowed. There are several different kinds of terriers, including Fox terriers, Boston terriers, Scottish terriers, and West Highland terriers.

Part C:
Read and Reason

My Terrier

Directions: Practice reading this poem with a friend. Don't forget to use expression. Go back and circle all the words that describe terriers.

My terrier's a dirty dog.

He thinks that he was born a hog.

He squeals, he grunts, he ruts about

with that square-cut hairy snout.

But that dirty dog—he is no pig,

his haunches and his head are big.

If he'd just get off that derrier,

he'd know he was a terrier.

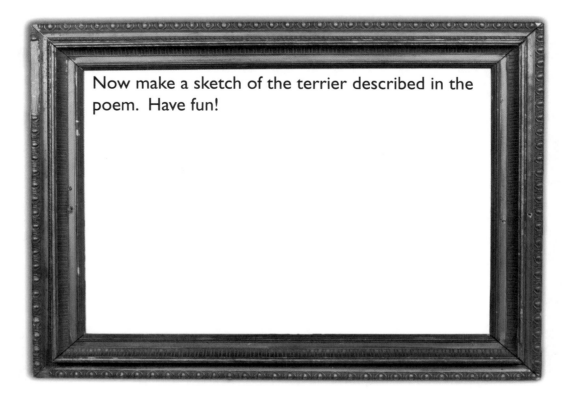

Now make a sketch of the terrier described in the poem. Have fun!

Part D:
Extend and Explore

Word Search

Directions: Find and circle the *terr* words listed below in the word search. Answers can be across, down, diagonal, or backwards.

SUBTERRANEAN   INTERMENT   MEDITERRANEAN
TERRAIN   TERRACE   TERRACOTTA
TERRITORY   TERRARIUM   TERRESTRIAL

Y	L	V	E	Z	P	P	J	J	D	N	M	P	W	L
F	S	T	X	T	I	I	S	D	E	I	J	K	A	T
P	G	U	T	N	E	M	R	E	T	N	I	I	Y	E
F	H	N	B	E	U	O	M	I	K	Y	R	X	R	R
Q	X	M	L	T	R	P	O	U	T	T	E	T	O	R
P	Z	T	T	K	E	R	H	C	S	L	E	M	T	E
Q	M	C	H	N	V	R	A	E	X	R	Z	L	I	S
M	W	U	L	D	Q	G	R	I	R	D	Z	L	R	T
M	E	D	I	T	E	R	R	A	N	E	A	N	R	R
X	H	F	Z	R	E	T	C	M	N	W	T	V	E	I
M	J	U	D	T	A	O	J	L	Q	E	N	S	T	A
A	D	S	R	K	T	R	T	E	R	R	A	C	E	L
L	R	T	U	T	F	D	R	S	V	A	E	N	I	T
C	X	O	A	J	M	V	F	E	L	I	E	R	P	Q
E	G	U	U	S	D	S	B	Y	T	I	N	B	G	M

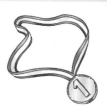

Part E:
Go for the Gold!

Magic Square

Directions: Match the words and definitions. Put the number of the definition in the correct box. If your answers are correct, each row and column will add up to the same number.

TERMS		DEFINITIONS
A. terrarium	2	existing outside the earth
B. extraterrestrial	3	burial
C. terrier	4	existing under the earth
D. subterranean	5	a porch
E. terra-cotta	6	clay for pottery
F. territory	7	a breed of dog
G. terrace	8	land
H. Mediterranean	9	container for raising plants
I. interment	10	_____ Sea

Magic Number: _____

A	B	C
D	E	F
G	H	I

Part A:
Meet the Root

Divide and Conquer

Directions: "Divide" words and then "conquer" them by writing the meaning of the prefix and base in the blanks. Then select the best definition. Words marked with an X have no prefix. Every word in this list is based on the base *trac, tract*, meaning "pull, draw, drag."

	prefix means	base means	definition
1. tractor	X		
2. contract			
3. retract			
4. attract	to, toward		
5. subtract			
6. extract			
7. detract			
8. distraction	in different directions		
9. attractive			
10. retrace			

Definitions

A. to appeal; to draw toward oneself
B. to pull out (a tooth, a splinter)
C. to take away from the looks of something; to lower the quality
D. a vehicle that pulls heavy equipment
E. a disturbance that draws one's attention in different directions
F. to go over one's path or tracks
G. to withdraw a statement; to take back one's words
H. appealing; drawing others toward oneself
I. an agreement drawing parties together; also, to pull together and tighten (as a muscle)
J. to reduce; to draw one number out from under another

Part B:
Combine and Create

A Secret Word

Directions: Use the vowels and consonants to make words that fit the clues. The secret word at the end uses all the letters.

Consonants: c d n r s t t
Vowels: a i o i

1. Move the head up and down ____ ____ ____

2. 2000 pounds ____ ____ ____

3. One of a constellation ____ ____ ____ ____

4. Piece of land (only one vowel) ____ ____ ____ ____ ____

5. Area that is part of a larger area, such as an area for police protection

____ ____ ____ ____ ____ ____ ____ ____ ____

Secret Word: something that draws attention away from what you are doing

____ ____ ____ ____ ____ ____ ____ ____ ____ ____ ____

DID YOU KNOW? 2+2=4

When we add numbers, we say that we add them "up": two plus two add up to four. But when we subtract numbers, we draw the lower number from under the higher number: two taken away from four is two.

DID YOU KNOW?

The English word *train* comes from the Latin base meaning to "draw" or "pull." A *train* is a series of cars on a track that are pulled by the main engine.

Have you ever seen a bride wearing a white dress with a long *train*? The *train* of a bridal gown is the long fabric that the bride "drags" behind her as she walks. A bridesmaid will often walk behind her and gather the *train* to keep the bride from tripping on it!

Part C:
Read and Reason

Poetry Work

Directions: Read this poem several times until you think you can read it smoothly and with good phrasing and expression. Think about the meaning of the lines as you read them. Then answer the questions below.

ATTRACTED TO TRACTORS?

My tractor has traction. It's ready for action.
It pulls and it pulls and it pulls.
When we pull two from ten, we call it subtraction,
a math process we learn in our -schools.
When we all pull together a contract is fashioned,
we agree to all play by the rules.
And when I'm pulled toward my books,
it's a kind of attraction.
I think books and reading are cool.

Questions:

1. On the line below, write what you think the word part *tract* means.

   _____

2. Write a sentence using the words *detract* and *pull*. _____

   _____

   _____

   _____

Part D:
Extend and Explore

Fill in the Blanks

Directions: Think of a *trac, tract* word that makes sense for each sentence.

1. Let's come to an agreement and sign a _____ (draw together).

2. The purpose of previews at the movies is to "draw" you "to" the same theater again next week. This is why we call them "previews of coming _____."

3. Have you ever had a dentist _____ (pull out) one of your teeth?

4. All the students chattering in the hallway _____ (pulled in different directions) my attention while I was taking the test. I could not concentrate.

5. I could not remember where I had left my book bag. So I went back and _____ (drew again) my steps.

6. The journalist had to _____ (withdraw or draw back) the statement he had written about the mayor.

7. I think movie stars are quite _____ (appealing): I feel "drawn" "to" them. Do you?

Now write your own sentences. Put a clue in for the missing *trac, tract* words. Share your sentences with a classmate. See if he or she can figure out the missing words.

8. _____

9. _____

10. _____

Part E:
Go for the Gold!

Sixteen Square Wordo

Directions: This game is like Bingo. First, choose a free box and mark it with an X. Then choose words from the list provided by your teacher and write one word in each box. You can choose the box for each word. Then your teacher will give a clue for each word. Mark an X in the box for each word you match to the clue. If you get four words in a row, column, diagonal, or four corners, call out, "Wordo!"

Divide and Conquer

Directions: Your teacher will give you a list of words. "Divide" each word into a prefix and a base. Then "conquer" them by writing the meaning of the words.

	word	prefix means	base means	definition
1.	_____	_____	_____	_____
2.	_____	_____	_____	_____
3.	_____	_____	_____	_____
4.	_____	_____	_____	_____
5.	_____	_____	_____	_____
6.	_____	_____	_____	_____
7.	_____	_____	_____	_____
8.	_____	_____	_____	_____
9.	_____	_____	_____	_____
10.	_____	_____	_____	_____

Part B:
Combine and Create

Sentence Writing

Directions: Write a sentence for each word pair. Include both words in one sentence.

1. terrier / spectacles

_____

_____

2. voice / spectator

_____

_____

3. subtract / vocabulary

_____

_____

4. trace / Mediterranean Sea

_____

_____

5. invoke / auditorium

_____

_____

Part C:
Read and Reason

Word Invention Riddles

Directions: Work with a partner to invent new *audi, voc, spect, terr,* or *trac* words.
Follow these directions:

1. Make up words using the bases *audi, voc, spect, terr,* or *trac.*
2. Choose one of your invented words to create a riddle.
3. Write the invented word.
4. Write three clues to help others figure it out.
5. One of the clues must describe the meaning of the prefix.
6. Choose one invented word riddle to share with the class. See if they can figure it out!

Here is an example:

Clues:

1. It swims in the ocean.
2. It also likes land.
3. It can be caught and fried for dinner.
   Invented Word: **terrafish**

Now you try it!

Clues:

1. _____

2. _____

3. _____

Invented Word: _____

Part D:
Extend and Explore

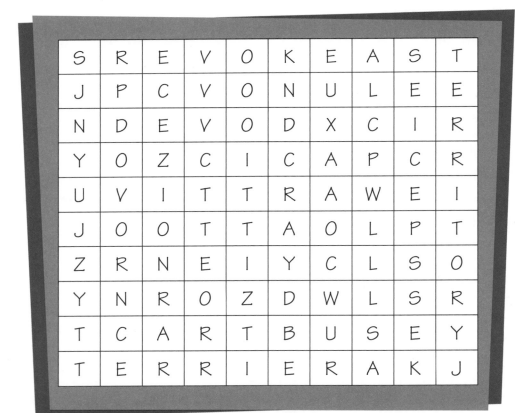

Word Search

Directions: Find and circle the words in the puzzle. Be careful! Some words start with the same letters. Answers can be across, down, diagonal, or backwards.

AUDITION	AUDITORY	RETRACE
REVOKE	SPECIES	SPECTACLE
SUBTRACT	TERRIER	TERRITORY
VOCAL		

S	R	E	V	O	K	E	A	S	T
J	P	C	V	O	N	U	L	E	E
N	D	E	V	O	D	X	C	I	R
Y	O	Z	C	I	C	A	P	C	R
U	V	I	T	T	R	A	W	E	I
J	O	O	T	T	A	O	L	P	T
Z	R	N	E	I	Y	C	L	S	O
Y	N	R	O	Z	D	W	L	S	R
T	C	A	R	T	B	U	S	E	Y
T	E	R	R	I	E	R	A	K	J

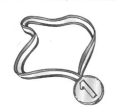

Part E:
Go for the Gold!

Magic Square

Directions: Match the words and definitions. Put the number of the definition in the correct box. If your answers are correct, each row and column will add up to the same number. One definition will not be used.

TERMS

A. inaudibly
B. vocalize
C. revoke
D. auditorium
E. inspection
F. prospector
G. terrace
H. terrarium
I. spectacular

DEFINITIONS

1 a tryout
2 speak out loud
3 amazing
4 a room for gathering
5 a porch
6 a close look
7 taking something back
8 someone who explores for mineral deposits or oil
9 can't be heard
10 a container for plants

A 9	B 2	C 7
D 4	E 6	F 8
G 5	H 10	I 3

Magic Number: 18

Part A:
Meet the Root

Divide and Conquer

Directions: "Divide" words and then "conquer" them by writing the meaning of the prefix in the blanks. Then select the best definition. Base meanings are provided. Every word in this list begins with the directional prefix *trans*, meaning "across, change."

	prefix means	base means	definition
1. transport	_____	*port* = carry	_____
2. transmit	_____	*mit* = send	_____
3. transfer	_____	*fer* = bear, carry	_____
4. transform	_____	*form* = form, shape	_____
5. transpose	_____	*pose* = put, place	_____
6. transit	_____	*it* = go	_____
7. transplant	_____	*plant* = plant	_____
8. transfusion	_____	*fus* = pour	_____
9. transgress	_____	*gress* = step	_____
10. transparent	_____	*par* = appearance	_____

Definitions

A. passage; the act or process of going from one place to another

B. to release and send (germs, waves, heat, light) across an area

C. to repot a plant; to plant an organ in a new body

D. to carry goods or people across an area

E. to switch the order of numbers or letters

F. an exchange of blood from one body to another

G. to violate a rule or commandment; to cross the line between right and wrong

H. to change schools; to change busses; to change from one place to another

I. clear and obvious; not opaque

J. to change shape or form; to alter significantly

Part B:
Combine and Create

Fill in the Blanks

Directions: Using the list of words in "Divide and Conquer" on page 64, fill in
the blanks with correct words beginning with the prefix *trans-*.

1. Every spring, we buy petunias in little containers from the nursery and
   _____ them to our garden.

2. The patient needed to have a complete blood _____
   after the surgery.

3. When I write "teh" instead of "the," I accidentally _____
   my letters.

4. When we moved from one school district to another, we had to
   _____ the credits from all my old courses.

5. The ancient Romans used boats to _____ their
   wares across the Mediterranean Sea.

6. My electric train has a special _____ that changes
   the form of the electric current from direct current to alternating current.

7. In large cities with heavy traffic, most people take the _____
   system to get to work.

8. If you sneeze without covering your mouth, you can _____
   germs to your classmates.

9. If I need to change busses while riding across town, I may ask the driver for
   a _____.

10. When a person steps across the line that separates right from wrong or
    commits an evil deed, he or she is guilty of a _____.

Part C:
Read and Reason

Word Meanings

Directions: Fill in the definition or write a sentence to match the definition.

1. transact — to conduct, as in business
   Sentence: _____

   _____

2. transaction — _____
   Sentence: Before the transaction could take place, the clerk had to scan all of my groceries.

3. transatlantic — _____
   Sentence: The first transatlantic flight took place in the early 20th century.

4. transfer — to move from one position to another
   Sentence: _____

   _____

5. transit — to go across
   Sentence: _____

   _____

6. transformer — _____
   Sentence: Since the transformer was down, everyone in the neighborhood lost electricity.

7. transgress — to pass beyond, commit an offense
   Sentence: _____

   _____

8. translate — _____
   Sentence: After I learned how to translate Spanish to English, I could understand more words and their meanings.

9. translucent — almost transparent
   Sentence: _____

   _____

Part D:
Extend and Explore

Word Search

Directions: Find and circle the words in the word search puzzle. Answers can be across, down, diagonal, or backwards.

TRANSACT	TRANSCRIPT	TRANSFER
TRANSGRESS	TRANSIT	TRANSMIT
TRANSNATIONAL	TRANSPLANT	TRANSPIRE
TRANSPORTABLE		

T	P	N	H	R	E	S	T	A	U	F	T	P	T	L
R	N	J	C	K	B	R	U	D	K	E	R	R	P	Z
A	O	A	P	T	A	E	O	J	R	V	A	Y	I	G
N	T	E	L	N	R	O	U	I	P	N	N	P	R	P
S	H	V	S	P	D	A	P	J	S	S	S	I	C	O
N	X	I	B	U	S	S	N	P	X	B	M	K	S	O
A	T	K	B	Y	N	N	O	S	O	U	I	Y	N	I
T	K	M	M	A	E	R	A	X	F	I	T	E	A	S
I	U	M	R	P	T	Y	P	R	O	E	C	W	R	A
O	Y	T	J	A	Z	D	O	V	T	Z	R	I	T	R
N	S	X	B	S	S	E	R	G	S	N	A	R	T	C
A	B	L	T	R	A	N	S	A	C	T	T	H	I	J
L	E	C	U	S	V	D	V	M	A	A	S	J	F	H
U	T	M	N	C	C	Q	M	B	V	X	O	L	B	E
E	T	Y	H	S	R	B	W	O	S	E	Y	M	O	B

Part E:
Go for the Gold!

Sixteen Square Wordo

Directions: This game is like Bingo. First, choose a free box and mark it with an X. Then choose words from the list provided by your teacher and write one word in each box. You can choose the box for each word. Then your teacher will give a clue for each word. Mark an X in the box for each word you match to the clue. If you get four words in a row, column, diagonal, or four corners, call out, "Wordo!"

Part A:
Meet the Root

Divide and Conquer

Directions: "Divide" words and then "conquer" them by writing the meaning of the prefix in the blanks. Then select the best definition. Base meanings are provided. Every word in this list begins with the directional prefix *inter*, meaning "between among."

	prefix	base word	definition
1. Internet	_____	*net* = net	_____
2. international	_____	nation	_____
3. interfere	_____	*fer* = carry, go	_____
4. interfaith	_____	faith	_____
5. intermural	_____	*mur* = wall	_____
6. interlude	_____	*lud* = play	_____
7. intercept	_____	*cept* = take, seize	_____
8. intermediate	_____	*medi* = middle	_____
9. interchange	_____	change	_____
10. interweave	_____	weave	_____

Definitions

A. music performed between the acts of a play; intermission or respite

B. a junction between roads and highways

C. occurring between schools (as in sports)

D. involving many nations and countries

E. to intertwine; to weave between the fibers of a fabric

F. to seize on the way from one place to another;

to take something from between a sender and recipient

G. involving many faiths and religions

H. the electronic network of computers among people and nations

I. occurring in the middle, between beginning and advanced

J. to meddle between parties; to intrude

Part B:
Combine and Create

Drawing Lesson

Directions: Draw each object in the boxes below.

Intersecting lines
Interlacing lines
Intercoastal waterway

DID YOU KNOW?

What does the *Internet* mean? The Internet refers to the enormous network of communication that takes place "among" the millions of people who use their computers. Just as fishermen might use a regular net to catch and hold huge quantities of fish, so the Internet is a vast creation that catches and holds great quantities of information. When we turn on our computers and access the Internet, we are able to communicate with countless numbers of people.

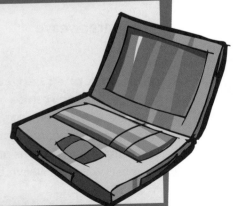

Part C:
Read and Reason

Advice Column

Directions: Read the following advice column and answer the questions.

Dear Adelia Advice,

I am writing to you to ask about the Internet. I want to know how to research zoo animals. I have to write a report on zebras. Can you help me?

Please Intercede

Dear Please Intercede,

I hope my advice reaches you before your report is due and does not interfere with your research. I would recommend doing an Internet search on zebras.

Adelia Advice

Questions:

1. What do you think _inter-_ means in the above advice column? _____

   _____

2. What does _interfere_ mean? _____

3. What does _Internet_ mean? _____

4. What does _intercede_ mean? _____

5. What advice would you give "Please Intercede" on how to research this topic? Share two ideas about how to find out information about zoo animals.

   One idea is: _____

   Another idea is: _____

Part D:
Extend and Explore

Writing Definitions

Directions: The *inter-* prefix means "between." What do these words have to do with "between"?

interrupt _____

_____

_____

interact _____

_____

_____

Internet _____

_____

_____

interagency _____

_____

_____

Part E:
Go for the Gold!

Crossword Puzzle

Directions: Read the clues and complete the crossword puzzle. Use the Word Bank for help.

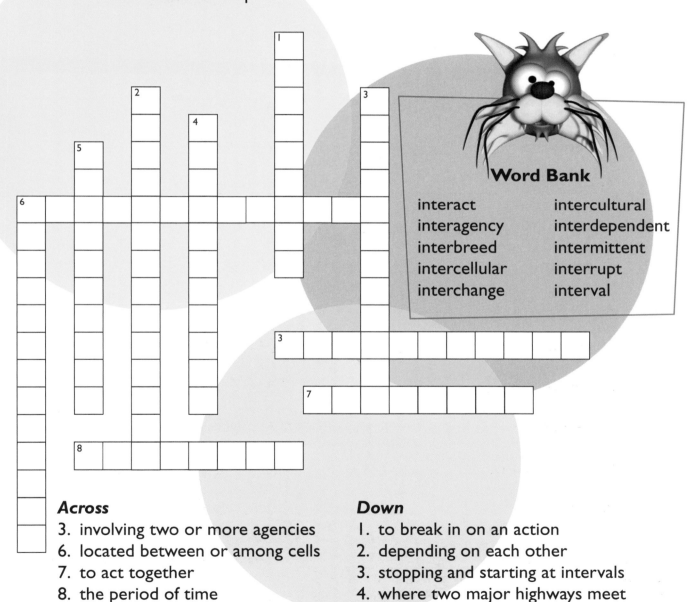

Word Bank

interact	intercultural
interagency	interdependent
interbreed	intermittent
intercellular	interrupt
interchange	interval

Across
3. involving two or more agencies
6. located between or among cells
7. to act together
8. the period of time between events

Down
1. to break in on an action
2. depending on each other
3. stopping and starting at intervals
4. where two major highways meet
5. to breed with another kind of species
6. between cultures

Part A:
Meet the Root

Divide and Conquer

Directions: "Divide" words and then "conquer" them by writing the meaning of the prefix in the blanks. Then select the best definition. Base meanings are provided. Every word in this list begins with the directional and intensive prefix *per-*, meaning "through, thorough(ly)."

	prefix means	base means	definition
1. permeate	_____	*me* = wander	_____
2. percolate	_____	*col* = strain, sieve	_____
3. perforate	_____	*for* = hole, opening	_____
4. persist	_____	*sist* = stand	_____
5. perfect	_____	*fect* = done	_____
6. permanent	_____	*man* = stay, remain	_____
7. perspective	_____	*spect* = look at, watch	_____
8. perfume	_____	*fum* = smoke, vapor	_____
9. perspiration	_____	*spir* = breathe	_____
10. permit	_____	*mit* = send	_____

Definitions

A. to punch holes through
B. vista; point of view, especially through a distance
C. sweat; moisture breathed through the skin
D. to endure through an effort; to stand firm in the face of warning or opposition
E. to drip through a filter or sieve

F. complete, accurate, and flawless; thoroughly done
G. to allow; a license
H. lasting and enduring; remaining throughout time
I. to soak through; to saturate
J. a fragrance that wafts through the air

Part B:
Combine and Create

Making and Writing Words

Directions: Use the vowels and consonants to make words that fit the clues. The secret word will use all the letters.

Consonants: m n n p r t

Vowels: a e e

1. A temporary place to sleep ___ ___ ___ ___

2. The opposite of far ___ ___ ___ ___

3. A fruit that grows on trees ___ ___ ___ ___

4. The hair around a male lion's face ___ ___ ___ ___

5. To primp (rhymes with "green") ___ ___ ___ ___ ___

6. A hobo, or to make big, loud steps ___ ___ ___ ___ ___

7. Trick or ___ ___ ___ ___ ___

Secret Word: lasting or enduring

___ ___ ___ ___ ___ ___ ___ ___ ___

DID YOU KNOW?

The English words *permit* and *permission* come from a Latin word meaning "to send through." When Roman farmers and soldiers would unleash their horses to roam through an open field, they *permitted* the animals to move freely in space by "sending" them "through" the area. Even today, we need *permission* from our parents to move about freely in certain areas. We may need a *permit* signed by our teacher to walk in the halls while class is in session.

Part C:
Read and Reason

Fill in the Blanks

Directions: Complete the paragraphs by using the *per-* words listed at the end.

We are making a new garden in our yard. We can't have any

_____ structures because they are not _____

in our neighborhood. We can plant flowers, though. I read about gardens on the

Internet. Experts recommend that 25 _____ of a garden should

be planted with _____ flowers. Their fragrance will

_____ the fragrance of the annual flowers, which must be

replanted every year.

➤ *percent, perennial, permanent, permeate, permitted*

I just love playing _____ instruments! I like them all, but

I think the tympani is my favorite. There's something about the way its sound

_____ a room. I practice nearly every day. I want to

_____ my playing, and my teacher tells me _____

like this will help me achieve my goal.

➤ *percussion, perfect, permeates, persisting*

Part D:
Extend and Explore

Word Search

Directions: Find and circle the words in the word search puzzle. Answers can be across, down, diagonal, or backwards.

PERAMBULATE   PERCENT   PERCEPTION
PERCOLATE   PERCUSSION   PERFECT
PERJURY   PERMEABLE   PERPETUAL
                    PERVASIVE

P	I	T	Z	R	J	E	R	B	P	B	Q	P	R	C
C	E	L	W	Q	E	I	C	E	X	A	P	E	I	S
E	Y	R	L	V	V	H	R	X	L	L	E	R	N	E
X	E	T	A	L	O	C	R	E	P	V	R	J	H	C
P	Z	L	Y	M	U	D	I	R	I	I	C	U	Y	H
S	E	J	B	S	B	I	P	S	Q	L	E	R	X	S
Z	P	R	S	A	A	U	A	Z	L	T	P	Y	S	P
U	Y	I	F	R	E	V	L	N	A	W	T	H	Y	Y
B	O	N	I	E	R	M	C	A	U	B	I	L	X	D
N	Q	W	M	E	C	K	R	B	T	Z	O	X	X	S
Y	W	Z	P	W	R	T	B	E	E	E	N	E	A	Y
P	E	R	C	E	N	T	H	S	P	E	V	B	N	L
X	I	K	B	R	N	Q	J	A	R	T	H	K	C	L
U	I	I	A	L	L	W	X	N	E	I	B	V	J	F
J	I	Y	P	I	N	L	D	Z	P	D	H	V	J	S

Part E:
Go for the Gold!

Magic Square

Directions: Work with a partner to complete the magic squares. If you are right, the "magic number" will be the same if you add across or down. Some definitions will not be used.

TERMS	DEFINITIONS
A. perspire	1 make a hole through
B. perspective	2 a tool for building houses
C. perambulator	3 break an oath by telling a lie
D. percent	4 grant a request
E. perspiration	5 a type of food
F. permission	6 a nonfiction book
G. percussion	7 skin breathes through your clothes
H. perjury	8 a baby stroller
I. permit	9 a kind of musical instrument
	10 100 _____ is a perfect score
	11 seeing something from many angles
	12 _____ stain
	13 a plant that grows outdoors
	14 seek a _____ to drive a car

A	B	C
D	E	F
G	H	I

Magic Number: _____

    #22648 *Building Vocabulary from Word Roots*

Part A:
Meet the Root

Divide and Conquer

Directions: "Divide" words and then "conquer" them by writing the meaning of the prefix in the blanks. Then select the best definition. Base meanings are provided. Every word in this list begins with the Greek prefix *auto*, meaning "self."

		prefix	base word	definition
1.	automobile	_____	*mobil* = move	_____
2.	autograph	_____	*graph* = write	_____
3.	automat	_____	*mat* = act	_____
4.	autobiography	_____	*bi(o)* = life; *graph* = write	_____
5.	autoharp	_____	harp	_____
6.	autopilot	_____	pilot	_____
7.	automatic	_____	*mat* = act	_____
8.	autocrat	_____	*crat* = ruler	_____
9.	autobiographer	_____	*bi(o)* = life *graph* = write	_____
10.	autohypnosis	_____	*hypno* = sleep	_____

Definitions

A. a type of restaurant with self-serve food, using coin-machines
B. self-induced hypnosis
C. one who writes his or her own life story
D. a signature written by one's own hand
E. a tyrant or dictator; one who rules by himself

F. a zither or harp that plays its own chords
G. the written story of the author's own life
H. a control or gear enable a plane to steer itself
I. a self-propelled vehicle (as opposed to a horse-drawn carriage)
J. self-acting; mechanical; spontaneous

Part B:
Combine and Create

Solving Riddles

Directions: Solve the riddles with *auto-* words.

1. I am a story.
    The author tells about his or her own life in me.
    I have word parts that mean "self," "life," and "write."

    _____

2. You write me.
    I am your name.
    Some people collect me from famous people.

    _____

3. I am an old-fashioned word.
    Today most people call me "car."
    I have a word part that means
    "self" and another one that has
    to do with moving.
    I have four syllables.

    _____

Part C:
Read and Reason

Limericks

Directions: Read the following limerick. Circle the *auto-* words. Then answer the questions.

I wrote a diary about my past
an autobiography at last
for sale at the mall
autographed real small
and I found out writing is a blast.

Questions:

1. Write what you think each *auto-* word means. _____

_____

_____

   Now, write what you think *auto-* means. _____

_____

2. Do you like to write? Explain why or why not. _____

_____

3. If you wrote a diary about *your* past, tell three things that would be in it.

   I would write about _____

_____.

   I would also tell about _____

_____.

   Finally, I would share about _____

_____.

Part D:
Extend and Explore

Word Meanings

Directions: Tell what these words have to do with "self."

autopilot_____

_____

_____

automobile _____

_____

_____

autograph _____

_____

_____

automatic _____

_____

_____

Part E:
Go for the Gold!

Sixteen Square Wordo

Directions: This game is like Bingo. First, choose a free box and mark it with an X.
Then choose words from the list provided by your teacher and write
one word in each box. You can choose the box for each word. Then
your teacher will give a clue for each word. Mark an X in the box for
each word you match to the clue. If you get four words in a row,
column, diagonal, or four corners, call out, "Wordo!"

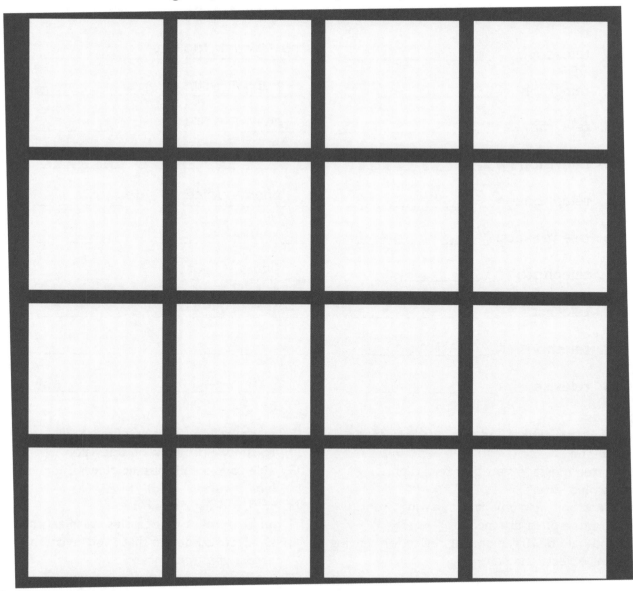

Part A:
Meet the Root

Divide and Conquer

Directions: "Divide" words and then "conquer" them by writing the meaning of the prefix in the blanks. Then select the best definition. Base meanings are provided. Every word in this list begins with the Greek prefix *tele-*, meaning "far, from afar."

	prefix means	base means	definition
1. telescope	_____	*scop* = watch, look at	_____
2. telegraph	_____	*graph* = write	_____
3. telegram	_____	*gram* = write	_____
4. television	_____	*vis* = see	_____
5. telephone	_____	*phon* = voice	_____
6. telemarketer	_____	market	_____
7. telephoto	_____	*photo* = light	_____
8. telecast	_____	*cast* = broadcast	_____
9. telethon	_____	X	_____
10. televise	_____	*vis* = see	_____

Definitions

A. one who advertises and sells products by telephone

B. a written message sent by a telegraph; an electronic letter

C. an electronic instrument for viewing events and programs from a distance

D. a hand-held or larger optical device for viewing distant objects and stars

E. an hours-long televised fundraiser

F. to show a program on television

G. able to focus on distant objects; a far-viewing lens

H. to broadcast on television

I. an instrument that carries voice across distance

J. an electrical device that sends written messages across great distances

Part B:
Combine and Create

Making New Words

Directions: Change the endings on these words to make new words. Make sure the new words contain *tele-*.

1. televise _____

    _____

2. telecast _____

    _____

3. telephone _____

    _____

DID YOU KNOW?

The popularity of the *telephone* and *television* resulted in two more *tele-* inventions. *Telemarketers* use the telephone to sell their goods and services, and *televangelists* use the television to preach.

DID YOU KNOW?

The prefix *tele-* is so commonly associated with *telephones*, *televisions*, and *telegraphs* that the letter "T" itself can be used as an abbreviation for them: the business name AT&T™ stands for American Telephone and Telegraph. The "T" in "TV" stands for television.

Part C:
Read and Reason

Limerick

Directions: Read the following limerick and answer the questions.

A telephone is a "talking-machine,"
and the telescope can see the night sky.
The telecaster reports
the news on TV.
A telegram is a message to you.

Questions:

1. What does *tele-* mean in the above limerick? _____

_____

2. Using the context clues from the limerick, define one of the *tele-* words in

the space below. _____

_____

3. Choose two different *tele-* words from the limerick. Use both of them in

one sentence. _____

_____

Part D:
Extend and Explore

Crossword Puzzle

Directions: Read the clues and complete the crossword puzzle.

Across

1. message sent by telegraph
2. receives pictures sent from afar
3. receives sounds sent from afar
4. makes far off objects appear closer

Down

1. camera lens for use with far away things
2. to show on TV
4. sends messages by electric signals

Part E:
Go for the Gold!

Sixteen Square Wordo

Directions: This game is like Bingo. First, choose a free box and mark it with an X.
Then choose words from the list provided by your teacher and write
one word in each box. You can choose the box for each word. Then
your teacher will give a clue for each word. Mark an X in the box for
each word you match to the clue. If you get four words in a row,
column, diagonal, or four corners, call out, "Wordo!"

Part A:
Meet the Root

Divide and Conquer

Directions: Your teacher will give you a list of words. "Divide" each word into a prefix and a base. Then "conquer" them by writing the meaning of the words.

	word	prefix means	base means	definition
1.				
2.				
3.				
4.				
5.				
6.				
7.				
8.				
9.				
10.				

Part B:
Combine and Create

What Doesn't Belong?

Directions: Cross out the word that doesn't belong in the group. On the lines,
write why it doesn't belong.

hypertension	intercoastal
transatlantic	transnational

_____

_____

_____

_____

_____

_____

_____

_____

Part C:
Read and Reason

Word Parts

Directions: First, make as many words as you can that have the word parts. Then tell what the word parts mean.

1. tele- + vis _____

   _____

   tele- means _____

   vis means _____

2. auto- + graph _____

   _____

   auto- means _____

   graph means _____

3. trans- + mit _____

   _____

   trans- means _____

   mit means _____

Part D:
Extend and Explore

Magic Square

Directions: Work with a partner to complete the magic squares. If you are right, the "magic number" will be the same if you add across or down. One definition will not be used.

TERMS	DEFINITIONS
A. interrupt	1 a tryout
B. automatic	2 working by itself
C. telescope	3 get in the way of
D. transatlantic	4 crossing the Atlantic Ocean
E. permit	5 send
F. percentage	6 allow
G. transmit	7 instrument that makes objects seem larger and nearer
H. automobile	8 portion
I. interfere	9 to break in on
	10 a car

A	B	C
D	E	F
G	H	I

Magic Number: _____

Part E:
Go for the Gold!

Word Search

Directions: Find and circle the words in the puzzle. Be careful! Some words start with the same letters. Answers can be across, down, diagonal, or backwards.

AUTOBIOGRAPHY   AUTOMATIC   INTERJECT
INTERRUPT   PERCENTAGE   PERSEVERE
TELEGRAPHIC   TELEPHONING   TRANSFER
     TRANSMITTAL

T	T	M	R	B	E	H	V	Y	J	P	Z	Y	D	C
E	C	E	P	F	L	R	B	Z	E	T	H	C	I	H
L	E	T	L	G	K	I	E	R	Y	P	Z	T	K	W
E	J	A	W	E	O	H	C	V	A	L	A	X	W	K
P	R	G	E	E	G	E	N	R	E	M	Y	S	R	Q
H	E	A	A	C	N	R	G	L	O	S	O	Y	D	H
O	T	R	Z	T	A	O	A	T	T	W	R	W	L	Q
N	N	E	A	J	I	T	U	P	F	Z	M	E	A	C
I	I	G	W	B	P	A	S	B	H	R	D	K	P	K
N	E	Z	O	T	R	A	N	S	M	I	T	T	A	L
G	M	T	R	A	N	S	F	E	R	U	C	G	T	X
W	U	G	B	Y	T	O	B	Y	Q	M	K	X	G	P
A	U	U	O	X	G	M	O	X	K	V	H	W	L	E
F	O	C	C	B	E	Z	O	T	J	F	Y	M	P	G
T	K	Z	Y	I	B	T	P	U	R	R	E	T	N	I

Part A:
Meet the Root

Divide and Conquer

Directions: "Divide" words and then "conquer" them by writing the meaning of the base and suffix in the blanks. Then select the best definition. Every word in this list ends in the suffixes -*ible*, -*able*, meaning "can or able to be done." **Hints:** Words #1 and #7–10 attach the suffix to a whole word; words #2–6 attach the suffix to a Latin base.

	base means	suffix means	definition
1. drivable	_____	_____	_____
2. portable	_____	_____	_____
3. flexible	*flex* = bend	_____	_____
4. credible	*cred* = believe	_____	_____
5. visible	_____	_____	_____
6. audible	_____	_____	_____
7. acceptable	_____	_____	_____
8. digestible	_____	_____	_____
9. convertible	_____	_____	_____
10. collectible	_____	_____	_____

Definitions

A. able to be digested
B. able to be changed or converted
C. able to be bent or twisted
D. able to be collected
E. able to be heard

F. able to be lifted or carried
G. able to be seen
H. able to be believed
I. satisfactory; able to be accepted
J. able to be driven

Part B:
Combine and Create

Word Chart

Directions: Add *-ible* or *-able* to each word. Then put each word on the chart.

absorb	accept	chew	collapse	collect	defend	digest

-able	*-ible*

DID YOU KNOW?

When inventors came up with a new kind of automobile whose top could go up and down, they wanted to give it a name that would attract customers. They went to the Latin language, searching for a word that meant "able to be changed from covered to uncovered." They found the word *convert*, which means "to change," and added the suffix *-ible*. They called their new invention the *convertible automobile*, which then became simply the *convertible*. What would you be more inclined to buy: a *changeable* car, a *roofless* car, an *uncoverable* car, or a shiny *convertible*?

Part C:
Read and Reason

Vocabulary Practice

Directions: Write definitions to help you understand each vocabulary word below. Sentences have been provided to give you clues. Then, pick the correct words to complete the sentences in 6–10.

1. admissible —_____

    Sentence: The judge ruled that the defendant's journals were not admissible in court.

2. defensible —_____

    Sentence: The defendant, however, proclaimed that his claims were defensible through his journal entries and should be allowed in court.

3. collectible —_____

    Sentence: Baseball cards and stamps are popular collectible items.

4. flexible — _____

    Sentence: Working flexible hours means that your schedule is different every week.

5. digestible — _____

    Sentence: I need to eat something digestible after feeling ill.

6. His voice was _____ (audible, visible), for he raised it louder so that he could be heard by everyone in the room.

7. John wanted to buy _____ (portable, washable) jeans because he worked in a garage and would get grease all over them.

8. Our new convertible had an automatic _____ (collapsible, defensible) roof.

9. The new technology is _____ (usable, digestible) only by those who are trained to use it.

10. The burnt popcorn was not _____ (edible, wearable), so I put it in the garbage.

Part D:
Extend and Explore

Word Search

Directions: Find and circle the words in the puzzle. Be careful! Some words start with the same letters. Answers can be across, down, diagonal, or backwards.

ABSORBABLE	ADMISSIBLE	BANKABLE
CHEWABLE	CORRUPTIBLE	DIGESTIBLE
EXPORTABLE	IRRESISTIBLE	PROGRAMMABLE
	WALKABLE	

A	C	E	F	G	L	G	F	E	R	O	I	E	N	T
B	D	L	Z	B	B	L	P	Z	G	R	X	I	Y	E
S	H	B	M	I	C	H	I	S	R	P	J	T	O	L
O	I	A	E	U	X	X	E	E	O	C	L	G	D	B
R	P	W	U	L	R	L	S	R	T	V	L	A	D	I
B	U	E	E	L	B	I	T	P	U	R	R	O	C	S
A	U	H	U	A	S	A	Z	D	Z	R	E	K	A	S
B	B	C	K	T	B	Q	M	K	E	N	T	W	Q	I
L	S	L	I	L	M	Q	O	M	Q	C	V	C	W	M
E	A	B	E	L	B	A	K	N	A	B	X	I	E	D
W	L	G	I	Q	U	W	G	W	I	R	B	R	X	A
E	D	I	G	E	S	T	I	B	L	E	G	M	X	K
C	X	V	X	V	N	H	X	Y	Z	K	C	O	V	B
G	M	D	Z	F	S	M	H	T	D	H	X	A	R	C
B	Q	S	M	V	U	B	K	V	A	D	F	K	K	P

Part E:
Go for the Gold!

Partner Pyramid Pairs

Directions: With a partner, choose one of the word pairs below. Each of you should take one of the words and make a word pyramid. Share your pyramids with each other and the class.

possible—impossible   visible—invisible

legible—illegible   flexible—inflexible

credible—incredible   lovable—unlovable

readable—unreadable   doable—undoable

washable—unwashable   acceptable—unacceptable

_____   (word)   _____

_____ (antonyms) _____

_____ (synonyms) _____

_____ (Define the word.) _____

_____   _____

_____   _____

(Write a sentence using the word.)   (Write a sentence using the word.)

Part A:
Meet the Root

Divide and Conquer

Directions: "Divide" words and then "conquer" them by writing the meaning of the suffix in the blanks. Then select the best definition. Base meanings are provided. Every word in this list ends in the Greek suffixes *–ology,* meaning "study of" or *–ologist,* meaning "studier of, expert in."

	base means	suffix means	definition
1. theology	*the(o)* = god		
2. musicology	music		
3. geologist	*ge(o)* = earth		
4. gerontologist	*geront* = elderly		
5. gynecologist	*gynec* = woman		
6. technology	*techn* = art, skill, fine craft		
7. zoology	*zo(o)* = animal		
8. biologist	*bi(o)* = life, living being		
9. astrology	*astr(o)* = star		
10. ecology	*ec(o)* = environment, house		

Definitions

A. the study of stars and their supposed influence on human affairs

B. the study of industrial and electronic arts that improve human life

C. the study of music

D. an expert in the life sciences

E. the study of animal life

F. an earth scientist

G. an expert in medical treatment of the aged

H. the study of God

I. an expert in women's health

J. the study of the environment

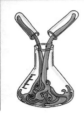

Part B:
Combine and Create

Fill in the Blanks

Directions: Here are some *-ology* words. Figure out the
words to fill in the blanks. Use the example to help you.

Ex. *Criminology* is the study of crime. A person who does this is called a *criminologist.*

1. *Climatology* means the study of _____. A person
   who does this is called a _____.

2. *Oceanology* is the study of the _____. A person who does this
   is called a _____.

3. *Musicology* is the study of _____. A person who does this
   is called a _____.

4. *Zoology* is the study of animals. A person who does this is called a_____.

Now answer these questions.

5. Which is the study of small living things?   biology   microbiology

6. *Psyche* is the mind. What is psychology? _____

7. Whose job is it to keep track of weather?   criminologist   climatologist

8. What is mythology? _____

Fill in the blanks.

9. *ge(o)* = earth / geology = _____

10. *bi(o)* = life / biology = _____

11. *hydr(o)* = water / hydrology = _____

12. *hemat* = blood / hematology = _____

Part C:
Read and Reason

It's Greek to Me!

Directions: Answer the questions by adding *-ology* and *-ologist* to these Greek bases.

anthrop	human being	*astr(o)*	star
myth	story	*ge(o)*	earth
archae	ancient	*the(o)*	god
entom	insect, bug		

1. Someone who studies long-ago civilizations is an

   _____ .

2. The study of bugs is called _____ .

3. Someone who studies the stars to predict the future

   is an _____ .

4. The study of people and their cultures is

   _____ .

5. The study of religion is called _____ .

6. Someone who studies rocks, volcanoes, oceans, and

   other parts of the earth is called a _____ .

7. The study of ancient civilizations is called

   _____ .

8. The study of stories and legends is called

   _____ .

9. An _____ studies people.

10. An _____ studies insects and bugs.

11. Which of these areas do you think you might like to study?

    Tell a partner.

DID YOU KNOW?

The English word *zoo* is an abbreviation. It stands for the long phrase, *zoological garden* or *zoological park.*

Zoology is the study of animals. People who specialize in zoology are called *zoologists.* When zoologists plan a zoological garden, they try to include animals from different regions of the world so that people who live in a city can have a chance to see these interesting creatures.

Polar bears, for example, do not live in the continental United States since our climate is too warm. You have to go to a zoo to see a polar bear.

Because a zoo contains so many different animals from all over the world, this same word can suggest a large and confusing collection of people. Have you ever gone to a crowded function that was noisy and disorganized? Have you ever been to a "zoo" of a party where everything was a crowded mess?

Part D:
Extend and Explore

Crossword Puzzle

Directions: Read the clues and complete the crossword puzzle.

Across
1. the study of climates
4. study of religion
8. the study of old age (Hint: *geront* means "elderly")
9. the study of life processes in nature
10. study of the earth

Down
2. study of people (Hint: *anthrop* means "people")
3. the study of music
5. the study of blood and blood producing organs (Hint: *hemat* means "blood")
6. applied science (Hint: examples include the computer and the Internet)
7. the study of diamonds and other precious stones (Hint: called "gems")

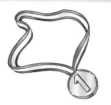

Part E:
Go for the Gold!

Sixteen Square Wordo

Directions: This game is like Bingo. First, choose a free box and mark it with an X. Then choose words from the list provided by your teacher and write one word in each box. You can choose the box for each word. Then your teacher will give a clue for each word. Mark an X in the box for each word you match to the clue. If you get four words in a row, column, diagonal, or four corners, call out, "Wordo!"

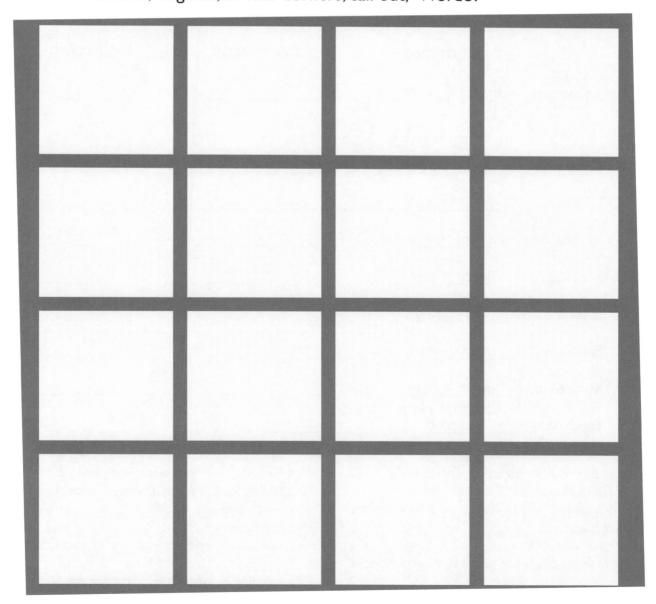

Part A:
Meet the Root

Divide and Conquer

Directions: "Divide" words and then "conquer" them by writing the meaning of the suffix in the blanks. Then select the best definition. Base meanings are provided. Every word in this list ends in the suffixes *-arium, -ary, -orium, -ory*, meaning "place, room."

	base means	suffix means	definition
1. aquarium	*aqu(a)* = water	_____	_____
2. terrarium	*terr* = earth	_____	_____
3. library	*libr* = book	_____	_____
4. factory	*fact* = make	_____	_____
5. laboratory	*laborat* = work	_____	_____
6. mortuary	*mortu* = dead	_____	_____
7. aviary	*avi* = bird	_____	_____
8. lavatory	*lavat* = wash	_____	_____
9. auditorium	*audit* = hear	_____	_____
10. sanctuary	*sanctu* = holy, sacred	_____	_____

Definitions

A. a room or building in which scientific work is conducted

B. a container for displaying small land animals and plants

C. a funeral home

D. a shrine; a place for housing sacred relics; a place of refuge and protection

E. a building or room containing books

F. a hall or building for hearing performances and speakers

G. a washroom

H. a container for displaying water and fish

I. a large structure that houses birds

J. a building in which products are made

Part B:
Combine and Create

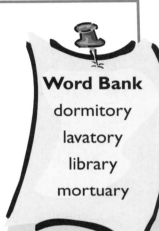

Answering Questions

Directions: Answer the questions using the words in the Word Bank.

1. Where can you find books to check out?

   _____

2. Where are dead people stored before their funerals?

   _____

3. What is another word for "washroom" or "bathroom"?

   _____

4. Where do college students stay and sleep?

   _____

Word Bank
dormitory
lavatory
library
mortuary

Figure out these words, too.

5. If *sol* means "sun," what is a solarium?

   _____

6. If *sanit* means "health," what is a sanitarium?

   _____

7. If *lavat* means "wash," what is a lavatory?

   _____

Part C:
Read and Reason

Word Bank

aquarium

auditorium

aviary

dormitory

lavatory

library

solarium

laboratories

Fill in the Blanks

Directions: Choose words from the Word Bank to fill in the blanks for the following story.

Last week I went with my family to visit the college where my sister will go to school next year. It was an amazing place. First we visited her _____. We saw the rooms where students sleep. They looked pretty big to me, but my sister is worried about whether she will have room for her _____. She really loves her fish and she wants to take them to school with her. We even saw the _____. It has six showers in it!

On the first floor of her dorm is a large _____. It's full of sofas and tables. It will be a great place for students to sit on sunny days.

We also took a walk around campus. We went to the _____. It is ten stories high. I bet it holds thousands of books. We also saw a huge _____ where my sister will take a class. Mom says several hundred other students will probably be in that class with her.

My sister is interested in science, so we spent time looking at _____. People were working in some of them, so we couldn't go in. Our final stop was the _____ because my sister likes birds almost as much as she likes fish. I saw a hummingbird and an eagle!

We really enjoyed our visit to the college. I can't wait until I am old enough to go to school there!

Part D:
Extend and Explore

It's Latin and Greek to Me!

Directions: Add *-arium, -ary, -orium,* or *-ory* to these Latin and Greek bases. Write what the new words mean.

1. *api* = bee(s) _____

2. *apothec* = storage _____

3. *aqu(a)* = water _____

4. *dormit* = sleep _____

5. *gran* = grain, wheat _____

6. *lavat* = wash _____

7. *libr* = book _____

8. mortu = dead _____

9. sanit = healthy _____

10. sol = sun _____

Which of these "room" or "place" words do you find most

interesting? Tell why. _____

_____

_____

Part E:
Go for the Gold!

Word Search

Directions: Find and circle these words in the word search puzzle. Answers can be across, down, diagonal, or backwards.

APIARY   APOTHECARY   AQUARIUM
DORMITORY   GRANARY   LAVATORY
LIBRARY   MORTUARY   SANITARIUM
                SOLARIUM

T	M	J	G	Q	F	E	Y	K	S	Y	H	C	G	O
C	U	E	Z	W	X	R	A	U	A	I	L	Q	N	T
S	I	N	W	S	A	P	A	P	N	E	M	J	W	Q
O	R	F	K	U	I	W	O	K	I	I	I	N	K	Q
S	A	V	T	A	E	T	K	L	T	W	V	G	N	G
Y	L	R	R	V	H	B	D	H	A	P	K	I	D	R
X	O	Y	L	E	C	O	U	E	R	Z	B	C	C	A
M	S	B	C	I	Y	R	O	T	I	M	R	O	D	N
Q	U	A	F	N	B	U	R	M	U	P	T	L	U	A
H	R	I	G	N	U	R	T	S	M	S	T	N	T	R
Y	X	N	R	K	V	L	A	V	A	T	O	R	Y	Y
M	P	C	E	A	Q	U	P	R	S	K	U	F	M	L
A	T	E	K	C	U	W	B	L	Y	C	P	X	A	H
L	K	V	D	H	T	Q	C	M	B	M	E	X	C	L
D	Q	H	G	A	H	X	A	W	V	E	K	H	I	T

Part A:
Meet the Root

Divide and Conquer

Directions: "Divide" words and then "conquer" them by writing the meaning of the base and suffix in the blanks. Then select the best definition. Every word in this list ends in the suffixes *-or, -er*, meaning "someone who does, something that does." Hint: All words in this list attach the suffix to a whole word.

	base means	suffix means	definition
1. employer	_____	_____	_____
2. sculptor	_____	_____	_____
3. actor	_____	_____	_____
4. computer	_____	_____	_____
5. teacher	_____	_____	_____
6. professor	_____	_____	_____
7. driver	_____	_____	_____
8. writer	_____	_____	_____
9. collector	_____	_____	_____
10. calculator	_____	_____	_____

Definitions

A. an adding machine that calculates mathematical sums
B. one who works with clay or sculpts stone
C. one who instructs or teaches
D. one who writes; one who composes a letter or other text
E. one who plays roles and acts them out
F. one who hires employees; a job-provider
G. one who operates a vehicle; one who drives for a living
H. an electronic device that computes information
I. a college or university teacher who professes advanced knowledge
J. one who collects keepsakes or special objects

Part B:
Combine and Create

Word Sketches

Directions: Make sketches and write an *-er* or *-or* word to go with your picture.

A person who dances	A person who rides
	A person who paints

DID YOU KNOW?

Some words we use today to describe things started out by describing people who performed certain tasks. As technology increased, some of these tasks were taken over by machines and special devices: the original *computer*, for example, was a "person who computes."

Poems

Part C:
Read and Reason

Directions: Read the two poems and then answer the questions.

The Who Does What? Poem

A collector and an auditor handle money, and
the batter and the dancer swing gracefully, and
the professor and the dictator lead successfully,
while
the actor speaks eloquently.

Questions:

1. Why is this poem titled "The Who Does What? Poem"? _____ _____

2. How are the batter and the dancer similar? _____ _____

The Obvious Who Does What? Poem

It's all in the word,
and
then
move forward.

A director
directs.

A driver
drives.

It's all in the word,
and
then
move forward.

A painter
paints.

A reader
reads.

It's all in the word,
and
then
move forward.

A runner
runs.

A sculptor
sculpts.

It's all in the word,
and
then
move forward.

A writer
writes.

A worker
works.

And, like I said,
It's all in the word,
and
then
move, move, move
forward.

Questions:

1. How does the poem help you understand what each person does?

_____

2. If we were to add "a teacher" to the above poem, what might the next line be?

_____

Part D:
Extend and Explore

What's in a Name?

Directions: At one time, people's jobs often became part of their last names. Here are some last names for people. Use them to figure out what kind of work someone in each of these families once did.

John Carver   was a _____

Mary Weaver   was a _____

Robert Cooper   was a _____

Ruth Miller   was a _____

Tom Sawyer   was a _____

Martha Cutter   was a _____

Nick Baker   was a _____

Alice Thatcher   was a _____

Luis Farmington   was a _____

Now think of some jobs you know. Make up names for people who hold them. Make sure the last name gives enough clues to figure the job out.

_____   was a _____

_____   was a _____

_____   was a _____

_____   was a _____

_____   was a _____

Which of all these *-er* and *-or* jobs seems most interesting to you? Tell why.

_____

_____

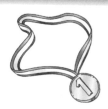

Part E:
Go for the Gold!

Crossword Puzzle

Directions: Read the clues and complete the crossword puzzle.

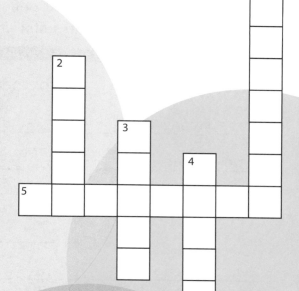

Across

5. one who produces
7. one who works
8. one who acts
9. one who writes

Down

1. one who collects
2. one who makes
3. one who rides
4. one who sculpts
6. one who teaches
10. one who drives

Part A:
Meet the Root

Divide and Conquer

Directions: "Divide" words and then "conquer" them by writing the meaning of the suffix in the blanks. Then select the best definition. Base meanings are provided. Every word in this list ends in the suffix *-ify*, meaning "to make."

	base means	suffix means	definition
1. fortify	*fort* = strong		
2. petrify	*petr* = stone		
3. verify	*ver* = true		
4. unify	*uni* = one		
5. pacify	*pac* = peace		
6. sanctify	*sanct* = sacred, bless		
7. testify	*test* = witness		
8. horrify	*horr* = frighten		
9. magnify	*magn* = big		
10. mortify	*mort* = dead		

Definitions

A. to make stronger; to strengthen against attack

B. to shock or appall; to make one's flesh bristle with horror

C. to bear witness; to make a legal declaration

D. to confirm; to check for truthfulness

E. to enlarge; to make bigger

F. to humiliate; to make someone "die" from embarrassment

G. to calm; make peaceful

H. to turn into stone; to make someone stone-cold with fear

I. to make one; to organize into a single whole

J. to bless or make holy

Part B:
Combine and Create

Matching Game

Directions: Match the definitions and the words.

_____ falsify   a. to make peace

_____ fortify   b. to frighten

_____ gratify   c. to make into stone

_____ magnify   d. to make solid

_____ pacify   e. to enlarge; to make big

_____ petrify   f. to make false

_____ solidify   g. to strengthen; to make strong

_____ terrify   h. to please; to make grateful

DID YOU KNOW?

When a person feels extremely embarrassed in public, sometimes he or she might say, "I was so embarrassed that I thought I would die!" They might also say, "I felt so bad that I wanted to curl up and die!" The Romans called this feeling *mortification* because the Latin base *mort* means "to die" (as in words like *mortal* and *immortal*). Of course, no one can die from public embarrassment! But when someone feels that bad they say they are *mortified*.

Part C:
Read and Reason

Making Sense

Directions: Put the correct *-ify, -ifier,* or *-ified* word in the blank. Remember that the sentence has to make sense, so choose the word that fits best!

1. The directions were not simple enough for us to follow. We asked the teacher to _____ them for us.

2. Did you notify them that we were coming? They said they were not expecting us because they were never _____.

3. I pacify a cranky baby with a _____.

4. We _____ our drinking water with a water purifier.

5. The teacher _____ the image with a brand new magnifying glass.

6. The runner _____ himself for the race with a hearty breakfast that included milk enriched with Vitamin D fortifiers.

7. Flowers _____ a yard wherever they are planted. They are natural beautifiers.

8. The man was sent to prison for making false statements, because it is illegal to _____ statements made under oath.

9. The lawyer wants me to _____ in court because another witness had testified to help the other side.

10. Dogs terrify most cats, but my cat was never _____ of dogs.

Now make up three sentences of your own. They should each include one *-ify, -ifier,* and *-ified* word. Choose from these words: glorify, dignify, unify, identify, mystify, personify.

1. _____

2. _____

3. _____

Part D:
Extend and Explore

Word Search

Directions: Find and circle these words in the word search puzzle. Answers can be across, down, diagonal, or backwards.

CRUCIFY   DEIFY   FALSIFY
FORTIFY   GRATIFY   MOLLIFY
MORTIFY   PACIFY   PETRIFY
                VERIFY

I	A	T	D	F	S	S	I	U	T	Y	R	P	T	T
Y	F	I	L	L	O	M	E	Q	E	F	J	Y	T	A
Y	F	I	R	E	V	M	W	K	A	I	S	R	U	T
E	N	Q	Y	N	Y	B	O	A	F	T	L	E	A	A
A	Y	P	T	T	B	F	F	J	J	R	G	N	M	M
C	Y	I	O	D	F	R	I	O	P	O	R	H	L	F
I	Z	W	R	Y	O	A	W	E	R	M	A	U	W	Z
S	Y	L	W	J	S	Y	D	T	D	T	T	B	O	E
H	O	F	B	A	F	D	P	I	C	B	I	T	O	K
E	J	D	I	I	T	A	F	G	T	H	F	F	U	G
L	C	O	C	R	C	O	J	J	E	Q	Y	M	Y	G
G	P	U	A	I	T	I	A	S	X	I	H	B	H	Z
C	R	S	F	R	D	E	X	V	B	D	S	G	J	M
C	Z	Y	K	E	V	D	P	Z	R	V	W	O	V	Y
F	X	W	R	N	F	A	L	S	I	F	Y	V	B	S

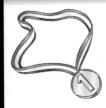

Part E:
Go for the Gold!

Sixteen Square Wordo

Directions: This game is like Bingo. First, choose a free box and mark it with an X.
Then choose words from the list provided by your teacher and write
one word in each box. You can choose the box for each word. Then
your teacher will give a clue for each word. Mark an X in the box for
each word you match to the clue. If you get four words in a row,
column, diagonal, or four corners, call out, "Wordo!"

Part A:
Meet the Root

Divide and Conquer

Directions: Your teacher will give you a list of words. "Divide" each word into a base and a suffix. Then "conquer" them by writing the meaning of the words.

	word	base means	suffix means	definition
1.				
2.				
3.				
4.				
5.				
6.				
7.				
8.				
9.				
10.				

Part B:
Combine and Create

Why Is It Different?

Directions: Talk with a partner about how these pairs of words are different. Write your ideas on the lines.

biology   biologist

_____

_____

pure   purify

_____

_____

admit   admissible

_____

_____

Part C:
Read and Reason

Odd Word Out

Directions: Work with a partner. Cross out the word that doesn't belong in the group of four. On the lines explain why the word doesn't belong.

collectible   insectology   laboratory   zoology

_____

_____

criminology   debatable   defensible   testify

_____

_____

auditorium   director   library   producer

_____

_____

_____

Part D:
Extend and Explore

Magic Square

Directions: Match the words and definitions. Put the numbers in the correct boxes. If you are correct, all the rows and columns will add up to the same number.

TERMS

A. collapsible

B. reproducible

C. favorable

D. geology

E. mythology

F. aviary

G. dancer

H. testify

I. ratify

DEFINITIONS

1 the study of the earth

2 one who sculpts

3 the study of blood

4 to give formal approval

5 something that is pleasing

6 to state a strong belief

7 able to be reproduced

8 the study of ancient myths

9 able to be collapsed

10 the study of humans

11 one who dances

12 a large enclosure for holding birds

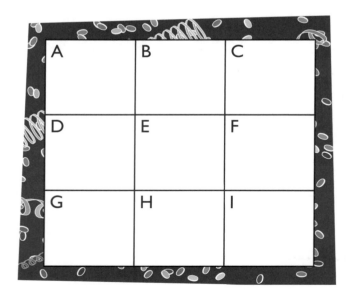

Magic Number: _____

Part E:
Go for the Gold!

Word Search

Directions: Find and circle the words in the word search puzzle. Answers can be across, down, diagonal, or backwards.

AUDIBLE	AUDITORIUM	BIOLOGY	COLLECTIBLE
DEFENSIBLE	INAUDIBLE	LABORATORY	LIBRARIAN
PRODUCER	READER	TESTIFY	

V	P	Y	M	X	L	P	J	C	O	E	V	C	Q	E
K	X	V	G	F	Z	M	O	W	Y	O	I	P	B	G
O	B	P	R	O	D	U	C	E	R	I	N	S	Z	U
T	R	K	O	C	L	T	P	G	O	N	O	Z	E	U
R	E	D	A	E	R	O	L	F	T	A	J	C	A	Y
K	A	S	T	L	F	B	I	B	A	U	V	Y	H	J
G	U	X	T	B	V	S	B	B	R	D	O	E	U	E
H	D	Q	U	I	Z	V	R	S	O	I	X	X	J	L
U	I	V	H	S	F	X	A	A	B	B	Z	N	I	B
X	T	J	B	N	T	Y	R	P	A	L	Q	L	G	I
C	O	L	L	E	C	T	I	B	L	E	S	W	P	D
E	R	Z	V	F	M	O	A	V	K	Q	L	J	Q	U
M	I	Y	U	E	R	G	N	R	Y	P	S	B	T	A
J	U	D	P	D	F	P	K	B	E	A	O	M	J	J
B	M	W	V	J	B	B	C	G	P	C	C	A	F	X

Part A:
Meet the Root

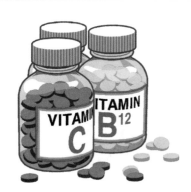

Divide and Conquer

Directions: "Divide" words and then "conquer" them by writing the meaning of the prefix in the blanks. Then select the best definition. Base meanings are provided. Every word in this list begins with the Latin prefix *multi-* or Greek prefix *poly-*, meaning "many."

	prefix means	base means	definition
1. multiply	_____	*ply* = fold	_____
2. multivitamin	_____	*vita* = life	_____
3. polygon	_____	*gon* = angle, corner	_____
4. polytheist	_____	*the* = god	_____
5. multicolored	_____	color	_____
6. multimillionaire	_____	million	_____
7. multilingual	_____	*lingua* = language	_____
8. polygamist	_____	*gam* = marriage	_____
9. polysyllabic	_____	*syllab* = syllable	_____
10. multimedia	_____	media	_____

Definitions

A. a person who marries more than one person at a time
B. a tablet containing many vitamins
C. to increase the number; to make many
D. using many means of communication to advertise or teach
E. one who believes in many gods

F. containing many syllables
G. one who owns many millions of dollars
H. a geometric figure with many sides and angles
I. having many colors
J. speaking many languages

Part B:
Combine and Create

Word Sorts

Directions: Put the words on the charts below.

| multimillionaire | multitude | multiply | multilateral |
| polyacid | polychrome | polygon | polypod |

describes living things	does not describe living things

| times | physical | big | visionary |
| shout | end | centipede | auditorium |

polysyllabic	monosyllabic

DID YOU KNOW?

In 1756, the word *Polynesia* was invented from two Greek words: *poly* which means "many" and *nesee* which means "island." It was used to describe a group of islands in the South Pacific Ocean. Why were these islands called *Polynesian*? There are "many" of them—in fact, more than 1,000! The Polynesian Islands form a triangle, with Hawaii, New Zealand, and Easter Island at each corner.

Part C:
Read and Reason

Fill in the Blanks

polyacid
polyangular
polychrome
polychromatic
multimillionaires
polygon
polynomial
polypod
multisyllabic
multicolored
polygraphical
polyharmony

Directions: Choose words from the Word Bank to fill in the blanks for the following sentences.

1. My new kaleidoscope has a _____ mirror system.

2. I ordered so many scoops of ice cream that the colors melted together and looked _____ as they dripped onto the floor.

3. Our science teacher told us that _____ is a phosphoric acid having more than one acid hydrogen atom.

4. She painted her shirt with a _____ rainbow so that everyone would notice how bright she felt inside.

5. Many _____ share their good fortune by spending their money to help others.

6. The picture in the math textbook explained that a _____ is a closed plane figure bound by three or more line segments.

7. Polytheism is a _____ word due to its many syllables.

Now choose three words you did not use to fill in the blanks above. Write one sentence for each word. Share your sentences with a friend. See if he or she can figure out the *poly* or *multi* word you chose.

8. _____

9. _____

10. _____

Part D:
Extend and Explore

Word Search

Directions: Find and circle the words in the word search puzzle. Answers can be across, down, diagonal, or backwards. Be careful! Some words start with the same letters.

MULTICOLORED   MULTILATERAL   MULTILAYERED
MULTIPLE   MULTIPLY   POLYACID
POLYGON   POLYPOD   POLYSYLLABIC

M	S	Q	P	E	C	A	Y	H	N	B	U	E	W	F
B	U	I	P	P	I	N	J	O	X	C	H	B	Q	K
B	Z	L	L	Q	B	W	I	Q	R	Y	U	K	I	R
W	O	Y	T	U	A	Y	G	W	V	L	M	E	J	U
O	N	M	X	I	L	W	U	J	Q	Y	E	V	S	N
C	D	E	R	O	L	O	C	I	T	L	U	M	D	S
B	D	E	R	E	Y	A	L	I	T	L	U	M	G	P
W	P	D	A	T	S	N	T	G	V	L	B	U	O	S
J	O	O	U	B	Y	O	D	E	T	B	F	L	L	C
X	K	R	L	H	L	G	F	I	R	U	Y	T	Q	G
I	Q	R	V	Y	O	Y	P	U	A	A	O	I	D	G
O	E	S	E	D	P	L	H	Q	C	P	L	P	H	K
S	C	U	Y	D	Y	O	B	I	J	D	C	L	U	P
L	H	B	T	L	E	P	D	B	S	T	U	E	U	E
S	G	M	A	V	E	H	E	S	R	N	L	G	F	S

Part E:
Go for the Gold!

Sixteen Square Wordo

Directions: This game is like Bingo. First, choose a free box and mark it with an X. Then choose words from the list provided by your teacher and write one word in each box. You can choose the box for each word. Then your teacher will give a clue for each word. Mark an X in the box for each word you match to the clue. If you get four words in a row, column, diagonal, or four corners, call out, "Wordo!"

Part A:
Meet the Root

Divide and Conquer

Directions: "Divide" words and then "conquer" them by writing the meaning of the prefix in the blanks. Then select the best definition. Base meanings are provided. Every word in this list begins with the Greek prefix *micro-*, meaning "small."

	prefix means	base means	definition
1. microbus	_____	bus	_____
2. microchip	_____	chip	_____
3. microcosm	_____	*cosm* = world	_____
4. microfiber	_____	fiber	_____
5. micromanage	_____	manage	_____
6. micrometer	_____	*meter* = measure	_____
7. microphone	_____	*phone* = voice	_____
8. microscopic	_____	*scop* = examine	_____
9. microworld	_____	world	_____
10. microwave	_____	wave	_____

Definitions

A. a very short electromagnetic wave
B. a soft manmade fiber; material made of such small fibers
C. the world as viewed from the microscopic level; the world of cells and tiny organisms
D. a group of tiny electronic circuits used in a computer
E. a small electronic device that increases the voice

F. a compact minibus; a very small bus
G. tiny; able to view only under a microscope
H. a small representative sample of a larger system; "the world in a nutshell"
I. a device for measuring extremely small distances and angles
J. to manage and control tiny details

Part B:
Combine and Create

Why Small?

Directions: Tell what these words have to do with "small."

microchip _____

_____

microscope _____

_____

microphone _____

_____

DID YOU KNOW?

The word *Micronesia* was invented from two Greek words: *micro-* which means "small," and *nes*, which means "island." It describes over 2,000 "tiny" islands in the Pacific Ocean that were created by volcanic activity that occurred millions of years ago. The Micronesian Islands are spread over three million miles between Hawaii and the Philippines in the North Pacific Ocean.

microsurgery _____

_____

_____

Part C:
Read and Reason

Story Time

Directions: Read the short story below and then answer the questions.

Have you ever heard the phrase "no two snowflakes are alike"? We know this is true, thanks to a man named Wilson Bentley. He spent his whole life examining and photographing snowflakes in the small town of Jericho, Vermont. As a young boy, Wilson examined snowflakes under a microscope. Although he grew up to be a farmer, Wilson spent years trying to figure out how he could photograph snowflakes by adapting a microscope to a camera. He was one of the first people to use a special camera called a *photomicrograph* that could take a small *(micro-)* object and use "light" *(photo)* to "write" *(graph)* a picture! In 1885, Wilson Bentley became the first person to capture the beauty of a single snowflake in a picture. During his lifetime, Wilson photographed over 5,000 snowflakes and discovered that no two were exactly the same. Because of his wonderful work with snow crystals, he was known affectionately as "Snowflake Bentley."

Questions:

1. *Photomicrograph* is made up of three Greek roots. What are they and what do they mean?

   _____ means _____

   _____ means _____

   _____ means _____

2. How can we be so sure that "no two snowflakes are alike"? _____
   _____

3. "Snowflake Bentley" found something he loved to do and made it his life's work. Do you have any hobbies or things you especially like to do? What are they? Could they become your life's work too? _____
   _____

Part D:
Extend and Explore

Limerick

Directions: Read the following limerick and discuss the definition of *micro-*. Practice the limerick so you can perform it for others in your class.

> My microworld is so tiny,
> microscopic to the 'nth degree,
> I can hide from all
> even in a wall.
> It takes a microscope to see me!

Writing Definitions

Directions: Choose a *micro-* word for each of these sentences. Then write a definition for the *micro-* word you chose.

microscope	microchips	microwave	microphone

1. I think I'll just pop a plate of yesterday's leftovers into my _____

   instead of cooking a big meal.

   Definition: _____

2. I could not hear the singer. She needed a better _____.

   Definition: _____

3. Computers are made up of hundreds of _____.

   Did you know that _____ can also be implanted in dogs

   to identify them?

   Definition: _____

4. "Snowflake Bentley" was a famous scientist and photographer who

   examined snowflakes under a _____.

   Definition: _____

Part E:
Go for the Gold!

Sixteen Square Wordo

Directions: This game is like Bingo. First, choose a free box and mark it with an X. Then choose words from the list provided by your teacher and write one word in each box. You can choose the box for each word. Then your teacher will give a clue for each word. Mark an X in the box for each word you match to the clue. If you get four words in a row, column, diagonal, or four corners, call out, "Wordo!"

Part A:
Meet the Root

Divide and Conquer

Directions: "Divide" words and then "conquer" them by writing the meaning of the prefix and base in the blanks. Then select the best definition. Every word in this list begins with the Greek prefixes *mega-*, *megalo-*, meaning "big." Hint: All words in this list attach the prefix to a whole word.

		prefix means	base means	definition
1.	megastore	_____	_____	_____
2.	megabucks	_____	_____	_____
3.	megapower	_____	_____	_____
4.	megalopolis	_____	*polis* = city	_____
5.	megavitamin	_____	_____	_____
6.	megastar	_____	_____	_____
7.	megawatts	_____	_____	_____
8.	megadose	_____	*dose* = give	_____
9.	megaphone	_____	*phone* = voice	_____
10.	megalomaniac	_____	_____	_____

Definitions

A. a person crazed by desire for big things; one deluded by a sense of greatness
B. a cone used to magnify the voice
C. a superstar
D. units of one million watts
E. a superpower; a country with global influence
F. a store that sells huge quantities and varieties of goods
G. an exceptionally large dose of medicine
H. an exceptionally large and powerful vitamin
I. a term for big money
J. a huge city

Part B:
Combine and Create

What Do You Know?

Directions: Answer the questions.

1. How are a *megaphone* and a *microphone* alike? _____
    _____

2. How are a *megaphone* and a *microphone* different? _____
    _____

3. What animal could be described as a *megapod*? (Hint: *pod* means foot.)
    _____
    _____

4. What animal could be described as a *micropod*? _____
    _____

5. If the doctor changed your medicine from a regular dose to a *megadose*,
    would you have to take more medicine or less medicine? _____
    _____

6. Who has more money, someone with bucks or someone with
    megabucks?_____
    _____

7. How do you think the *megamouth* shark got its name? _____
    _____
    _____

8. A regular city could be called a *metropolis*. What is a *megalopolis*?
    _____
    _____

Part C:
Read and Reason

Advice Column

Directions: Fill in the following blanks for the advice column letter and response. Then answer the questions.

Dear Adelia Advice,

My dad won the lottery and told me that we now had "_____" (megabytes, megabucks), which he said meant that we have large amounts of cash. But I don't know what all that means. Can you explain it to me?

Your Reader,

Money Matters

Dear Money Matters,

Having lots of money can be a _____ (megalopolis, megadose) of change. It means that you have so much money that your world changes overnight. So be ready, Money Matters, and be true to yourself while you go through this new change in your life. Money can bring _____ (megapower, megawatts), and you want to use that power wisely. Be sure to remind your dad of this as he spends his new wealth.

Adelia Advice

Questions:

1. Explain what Adelia Advice means when she tells Money Matters that she should "use her new power wisely."

   _____

   _____

2. Can you think of three things you might spend your money on if you won the lottery? Tell what they are and explain why it would be a good way to spend your money.

   _____

   _____

Part D:
Extend and Explore

Solving Riddles

Directions: Answer the riddles. Each one will be a *mega-* word.

1. I am a computer word.
   My abbreviation is MB.
   My last syllable rhymes with "light."   _____

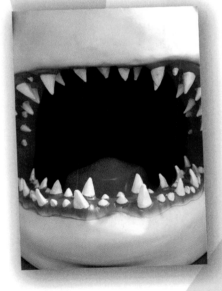

2. I am a kind of shark.
   I got my name because my mouth
   is very big.

   _____

3. You can talk through me.
   I will make your voice sound louder.
   I am round at both ends.
   My top is much smaller than my bottom.   _____

4. I am a slang word.
   I mean "a lot of money."
   I have three syllables.   _____

Part E:
Go for the Gold!

Sixteen Square Wordo

Directions: This game is like Bingo. First, choose a free box and mark it with an X.
Then choose words from the list provided by your teacher and write
one word in each box. You can choose the box for each word. Then
your teacher will give a clue for each word. Mark an X in the box for
each word you match to the clue. If you get four words in a row,
column, diagonal, or four corners, call out, "Wordo!"

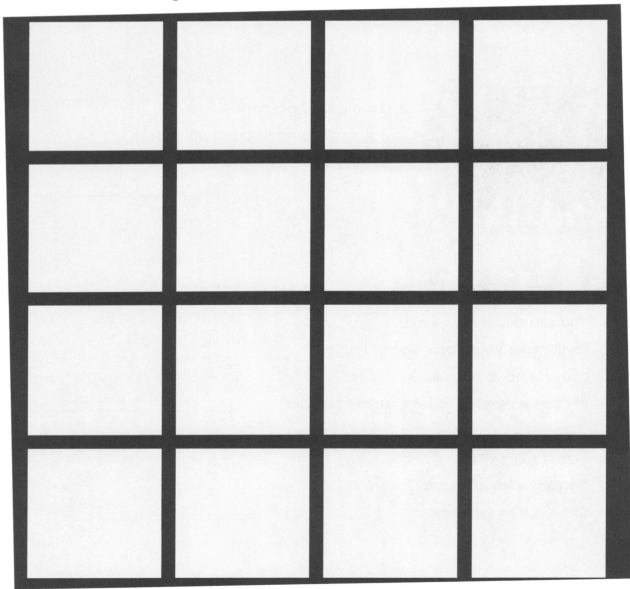

Part A:
Meet the Root

Divide and Conquer

Directions: Your teacher will give you a list of words. "Divide" words into base adjectives and suffixes. Then "conquer" them by writing the meaning of the words.

word	base adjective	suffix means	definition
1. _____	_____	_____	_____
2. _____	_____	_____	_____
3. _____	_____	_____	_____
4. _____	_____	_____	_____
5. _____	_____	_____	_____
6. _____	_____	_____	_____
7. _____	_____	_____	_____
8. _____	_____	_____	_____
9. _____	_____	_____	_____
10. _____	_____	_____	_____

Part B:
Combine and Create

Unscrambling the Letters

Directions: Unscramble the words.

These words will begin with the *micro*- prefix.

1. A very small ray of light is a _____.

m i a b e m c o r

2. A tiny piece that goes in a computer is a _____.

c c h i i m o p r

3. A very tiny thread is a _____.

b c e f i i m o r r

These words will begin with *mega*- or *megalo*-.

4. A store that sells many, many things is called a _____.

a e e g m o r s t

5. Cheerleaders use this device for
making their voices sound louder _____.

a e e g h m o n p

Now try these *multi*- or *poly*- words.

6. When I decide that 2 X 3 = 6, I am _____.

i i g l l m n p t u y

7. A centipede is a _____ because it has many feet.

d l o o p p y

Part C:
Read and Reason

More Writing Riddles

Directions: Go back through the words in this unit. Select three to use to make riddles. Write the riddles. Then see if a classmate can solve them.

_____

_____

_____

_____

_____

_____

_____

_____

_____

_____

Part D:
Extend and Explore

Word Search

Directions: Find and circle the words in the word search puzzle. Answers can be across, down, diagonal, or backwards. Be careful! Some words start with the same letters.

MEGALOPOLIS   MEGAPHONE   MEGASTORE   MICROFIBER
MICROSCOPIC   MULTICOLORED   MULTILAYERED   MULTIPLE
MULTIPLY   POLYGON   POLYPOD   POLYSYLLABIC

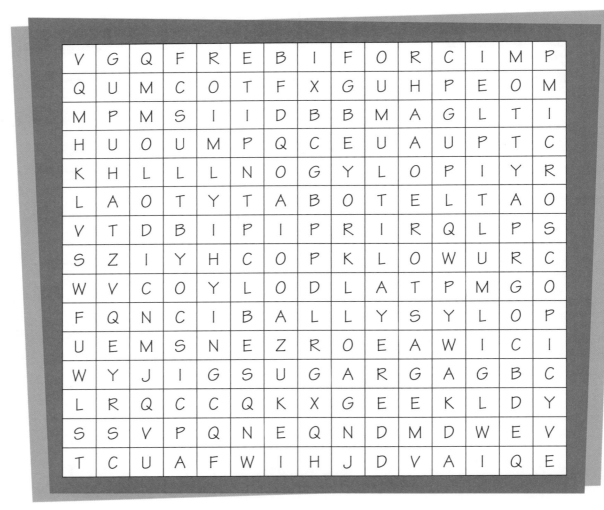

V	G	Q	F	R	E	B	I	F	O	R	C	I	M	P
Q	U	M	C	O	T	F	X	G	U	H	P	E	O	M
M	P	M	S	I	I	D	B	B	M	A	G	L	T	I
H	U	O	U	M	P	Q	C	E	U	A	U	P	T	C
K	H	L	L	L	N	O	G	Y	L	O	P	I	Y	R
L	A	O	T	Y	T	A	B	O	T	E	L	T	A	O
V	T	D	B	I	P	I	P	R	I	R	Q	L	P	S
S	Z	I	Y	H	C	O	P	K	L	O	W	U	R	C
W	V	C	O	Y	L	O	D	L	A	T	P	M	G	O
F	Q	N	C	I	B	A	L	L	Y	S	Y	L	O	P
U	E	M	S	N	E	Z	R	O	E	A	W	I	C	I
W	Y	J	I	G	S	U	G	A	R	G	A	G	B	C
L	R	Q	C	C	Q	K	X	G	E	E	K	L	D	Y
S	S	V	P	Q	N	E	Q	N	D	M	D	W	E	V
T	C	U	A	F	W	I	H	J	D	V	A	I	Q	E

A Final Reflection

Part E:
Go for the Gold!

Directions: Congratulations! You have finished this whole book! Now look back and choose the three roots you liked best. Write them down and tell why they are your favorites!

My Favorite Roots

1. _____

   I like this root because _____.

2. _____

   I like this root because _____.

3. _____

   I like this root because _____.

Now pick out three new words you learned that you think are really interesting. Write the words, and tell why they are your favorites.

Most Interesting Words

1. _____

   I think this is an interesting word because _____

   _____ .

2. _____

   I think this is an interesting word because _____

   _____ .

3. _____

   I think this is an interesting word because _____

   _____ .

Now compare your choices with those of your friends! Did you pick any of the same roots and interesting words?

 # 22648 Building Vocabulary from Word Roots